The
HIDDEN PLACES
of
WILTSHIRE

Edited by
Shane Scott

.   Published by:
Travel Publishing Ltd
7a Apollo House, Calleva Park
Aldermaston, Berks, RG7 8TN

ISBN 1-902-00714-X

© Travel Publishing Ltd 1997

First Published: *1995*
Second Edition: *1997*

Regional Titles in the Hidden Places Series:

Channel Islands	Devon & Cornwall
Dorset, Hants & Isle of Wight	East Anglia
Gloucestershire	Heart of England
Lancashire & Cheshire	Lake District & Cumbria
North Wales	Northumberland & Durham
Peak District	Potteries
Somerset	South East
South Wales	Thames & Chilterns
Welsh Borders	Wiltshire
Yorkshire & Humberside	

National Titles in the Hidden Places Series:

England	Ireland
Scotland	Wales

Printing by: Nuffield Press, Abingdon
Cartography by: Estates Publications, Tenterden, Kent
Line Drawings: Sarah Bird
Editor: Shane Scott
Cover : Clare Hackney
> Born in 1961, Clare was educated at West Surrey College of Art and Design
> as well as studying at Kingston University. She runs her own private water-
> colour school based in Surrey and has exhibited both in the UK and interna-
> tionally. The cover is taken from an original water-colour of the White Horse
> at Westbury Hill.

Foreword

The Hidden Places series is a collection of easy to use travel guides taking you, in this instance, on a relaxed but informative tour through the beautiful countryside of Wiltshire. Our books contain a wealth of interesting information on the history, the countryside, the towns and villages and the more established places of interest in the county. But they also promote the more secluded and little known visitor attractions and places to stay, eat and drink many of which are easy to miss unless you know exactly where you are going.

We include hotels, inns, restaurants, public houses, teashops, various types of accommodation, historic houses, museums, gardens, garden centres, craft centres and many other attractions throughout Wiltshire. Most places have an attractive line drawing and are cross-referenced to coloured maps found at the rear of the book. We do not award merit marks or rankings but concentrate on describing the more interesting, unusual or unique features of each place with the aim of making the reader's stay in the local area an enjoyable and stimulating experience.

Whether you are a visiting Wiltshire for business or pleasure or in fact are living in the county we do hope that you enjoy reading and using this book. We are always interested in what readers think of places covered (or not covered) in our guides so please do not hesitate to use the reader reaction forms provided to give us your considered comments. We also welcome any general comments which will help us improve the guides themselves. Finally if you are planning to visit any other corner of the British Isles we would like to refer you to the list of other *Hidden Places* titles to be found at the rear of the book.

Contents

CHAPTER ONE
Salisbury to Stonehenge

East End of Salisbury Cathedral

1
Salisbury to Stonehenge

Salisbury   *Map 4 ref F10*
18 miles SW of Andover on the A30

The beautiful medieval city of Salisbury stands at the confluence of the rivers Avon, Wylye, Bourne and Nadder. Originally called New Sarum, the settlement grew up around the present cathedral which was erected between 1220 and 1258 in a sheltered position two miles to the south of its Norman predecessor at Old Sarum. Over the centuries, the townspeople followed the clergy down from the wind-swept hilltop site on the edge of Salisbury Plain and the new settlement developed into a flourishing ecclesiastical and market centre which continues to host a twice-weekly open-air market every Tuesday and Saturday.

The new **Salisbury Cathedral** was the inspiration of Bishop Herbert Poole who wanted to distance the church from the military authorities occupying the great castle at **Old Sarum**. Sadly, the bishop died before his dream could be realised and it fell to his brother Richard to see the project through to completion. Work began on Easter Monday 1220 and continued for 38 years, a remarkably short time considering the scale of the building and construction methods of the day. As a result, this is the only medieval cathedral in England to be built entirely in Early English style.

The soaring spire rises to a height of 404ft, making it the tallest in the country. A remarkable architectural achievement, its central piers stand on foundations which go down less than ten feet into

Salisbury Cathedral

marshy ground. A brass plate set into the floor beneath the spire bears the inscription, *"AD 1737 Centre of the Tower"*. This commemorates the fact that fifty years before, Sir Christopher Wren had been brought in by the cathedral authorities who were concerned the spire may topple over. He calculated the structure was indeed leaning almost two and a half feet off-centre and his answer was to attach iron tie-rods to certain parts of it. When these were replaced in the 1950s, it was discovered Wren's efforts had been successful and the lean had not worsened in over 250 years.

The cathedral is said to contain a door for each month, a window for each day and a column for each hour of the year (making 8760 columns in all). The elaborately decorated west front incorporates a series of niches. At one time, each of these contained a carved figure but sadly, most of the original statues have been destroyed by weathering and those that remain are largely 19th-century copies.

A small statue of Salisbury's 17th-century **Boy Bishop** stands inside the cathedral's west door. It was a custom at that time for the choristers to elect one of their number bishop for a period lasting from St Nicholas Day to Holy Innocents' Day (6-28 December). One year, however, the incumbent is reputed to have been literally *"tickled to death"* by the other choirboys, and as a result of him having died in office, a statue was erected showing him in full bishop's regalia.

The oldest working clock in Britain, and possibly in the world, is situated in the cathedral's fan-vaulted north transept. It was built in 1386 to strike the hour and has no clock face. Also worth noting are the now-restored 13th-century roof paintings in the choir, and the 200 or so carved stone figures illustrating scenes from the Old Testament which line the walls of the octagonal chapter house.

The cathedral also contains a number of magnificent tombs, the oldest of which is that of the Earl of Salisbury, William Longespere, whose reclining armour-clad effigy has lain here since 1226. Eleven years before, the Earl witnessed the sealing of the Magna Carta by his half-brother, King John, and indeed one of the four remaining originals of this historic document is on permanent display in the chapter house. This is located in the library above the east walk of the cathedral's magnificent cloisters, the largest of their kind in England.

As the cathedral was built before the town, new accommodation had to be built to house the clergy and ancillary staff. This was constructed around a walled square which is now considered to be the finest cathedral close in the country. To enter the close it is necessary to pass through one of its medieval gateways, such as the Harnham Gate to the south or St Ann's Gate to the east.

Just to the south of the cathedral lies the **Bishop's Palace** which dates from the 13th century and now houses the cathedral choir school. During the Great Plague of 1665, Charles II based his court here for several months in order to steer clear of the pestilence which was sweeping London. The bishop's residence was also made famous by John Constable who painted his renowned landscape of Salisbury Cathedral in the palace gardens; the painting now hangs in the Victoria and Albert Museum in London.

The award-winning **Salisbury and South Wiltshire Museum** is situated in the 17th-century **King's House** on the western side of the cathedral close. This absorbing museum contains a large collection of historic artefacts, including relics from Stonehenge, pottery fragments from Old Sarum and sections of an ancient Roman mosaic. Special exhibits include the celebrated Monkton Deverill gold torc, the Pitt Rivers collection, and a series of watercolours by William Turner. There is also an interesting display of English china, pottery and glassware, and a mounted group of great bustards, the majestic birds which at one time could be found on Salisbury Plain. (Open Mondays to Saturdays and summer Sunday afternoons, 10am to 5pm, all year round.)

A few doors away, the Royal Gloucestershire, Berkshire and Wiltshire Regiment's Museum is housed in the splendid **Bishop's Wardrobe**, a building dating from the mid 13th century which was originally used to store the bishop's clothes and documents. The museum contains an interesting collection of uniforms, medals, pictures and regimental militaria which documents the history of the counties' infantry regiments since 1743. (Open daily, 10am to 4.30pm between April and October, plus weekdays in March and November; closed December and January.)

One of the most elegant buildings in the cathedral close can be found on the northern side of Choristers' Green. A superb example of Queen Anne architecture, **Mompesson House** was constructed for the wealthy Wiltshire merchant, Charles Mompesson, around 1701. Now owned by the National Trust, the property contains a delicately carved oak staircase, a splendid collection of period furniture and some fine overmantels and plaster ceilings which were installed by Charles Longeville around 1740. The Turnbull Collection of 18th-century English china and glassware is also housed here, and to the rear, there is a delightful walled garden with an attractive tearoom. (Open daily except Thursdays and Fridays, 12 noon to 5.30pm between late March and early November.)

Originally a 13th-century canonry, **Malmesbury House** on the northwestern side of the cathedral close was enlarged in the 14th century and again in the late 17th century when the west facade was added by Sir Christopher Wren to accommodate rooms displaying magnificent rococo plasterwork. The many famous visitors to the house include King Charles II and Handel who used to give recitals in the chapel above St Ann's Gate. The house contains some fine 18th-century furnishings is now the residence of the Cordle family. (Open Tuesdays to Saturdays, 10.30am to 5.30pm between April and end-September for guided tours.)

Mompesson House

A row of handsome 17th-century almshouses can be seen nearby which were built on the instructions of the Bishop Seth Ward. A walk around the centre of Salisbury reveals an unusual concentration of historic inns, shops and residential buildings which chronicle the city's development from the 13th century to the present day. A wonderful assortment of black and white half-timbering, overhanging gables and bow-windowed fronts, one of the most distinctive examples can be found in Queen Street the three-storey house built in 1425 for six-times mayor John A'Port. Restoration of this impressive timber-framed structure during the 1930s revealed that, remarkably, none of its original 15th-century timbers needed replacing. The building now houses the celebrated retailer, ***Watsons of Salisbury***, a state of affairs which allows visitors to inspect the interior, with its fine Jacobean wood panelling, stone fireplace and carved oak mantelpiece, whilst viewing their outstanding range of china and glass.

Watsons of Salisbury

It was in 1834, during the reign of William IV, that the firm of Watson and Co began offering fine china and glass to the people of Salisbury. Now over a century and a half later, they have greatly extended their service and enjoy connections all over the world. For the first 95 years, the business was located in ***Ye Halle of John Halle***, built in 1470 and situated in New Canal, Salisbury. However, in the late 1920s it became necessary to acquire new premises and by chance, ***Ye House of John A'Port*** in Queen Street became available.

This impressive Tudor building was carefully restored and the business was soon able to offer an even wider range of merchandise than before. As stockists of all leading manufacturers of china and glass, Watsons endeavour to fulfil the varied and exacting requirements of their worldwide clientele. A truly interesting building with many attractive goods on sale, Watsons of Salisbury should not be missed. *Watsons of Salisbury, 8-9 Queen Street, Salisbury, Wiltshire Tel: 01722 320311 Fax: 01722 412903*

Other notable buildings in the city are the octagonal **Poultry Cross**, which was constructed in the 15th century to provide shelter for market traders, and the nearby **Church of St Thomas of Canterbury**, which stands on the site of an earlier church which was completed twenty years before the cathedral. The present building contains a highly unusual 16th-century wall-painting which is situated above the chancel arch. Restored in the 19th century, this remarkable primitive work depicts Christ on a rainbow, accompanied by the Virgin Mary, St John the Baptist and a whole host of saints condemning the unworthy to eternal damnation. A city with great antiquity, even Salisbury's local cinema is housed in a former merchants' hall dating from the 15th century.

Red Lion Hotel

Two of Salisbury's loveliest old coaching inns can be found in the heart of the city. The famous **Red Lion Hotel** is set back from the road in Milford Street, and as visitors walk across the beautiful creeper-clad courtyard towards the entrance, they can truly appreciate the remarkable half-timbered exterior of this charming and historic establishment. Possibly the oldest continually-running purpose-built hotel in the country, it was originally constructed to house draughtsmen working on the new cathedral. Following the completion of the building in the late 13th-century, the White Bear as it was then known, became a popular lodging place for visitors to the magnificent new centre of worship.

Throughout the 17th century, the inn was owned by the Ray family, then as east-west road traffic increased in the mid 18th century, it became a main centre of activity for mail coaches operating between London and the West Country. Around that time its name was changed to the Red Lion, and during the following centuries, it became an important stopping place for people journeying across southern England on business. The Red Lion Hotel has now been owned by the same family for nearly 100 years.

It continues to welcome guests from near and far, and whilst great care has been taken to preserve its traditional character, many modern facilities have been incorporated into the framework of the original building which houses the reception, lounge, restaurant, bar and some delightful individually-decorated bedrooms. The hotel boasts an impressive collection of antiques, including some particularly fine Parliament clocks and, most notably, the rare skeleton and organ clock in the reception hall. The delightful atmosphere in the restaurant is enhanced by a much-admired china collection. One of its walls is constructed of wattle and daub which thought to date from around 1220.

Renowned for its traditional English and continental cuisine, the chefs pride themselves on a high standard of cuisine and, as in all areas of the hotel, the service is both friendly and attentive. The bedrooms all have en suite facilities and are individually decorated with both character and style. They are luxuriously furnished and provide for a most comfortable holiday or overnight stay. For honeymoons, anniversaries and other special occasions, the hotel has two superb rooms with antique four-poster beds, as well as a spacious suite overlooking the vine and flower-filled courtyard. The proprietor, Mr Michael Maidment, and his staff extend the very warmest of welcomes at this historic establishment which is superb in every way. *Red Lion Hotel, Milford Street, Salisbury, Wiltshire Tel: 01722 323334 Fax: 01722 325756*

The **Coach and Horses** in Winchester Street lays claim to being Salisbury's oldest inn. An important coaching terminus for several centuries, it was sold as the Talbot with two other properties in 1560 when the three buildings changed hands for just £38 10s 6d. In 1986, this delightful old building was completely restored: the interior was refurbished and brought up to the standard of a modern pub and eating place, while at the same time great care was taken to retain its original character and atmosphere.

Another concession to the modern age was the installation of one of the most advanced kitchens to be found in this type of establishment. Chef proprietors Martin and Angie Cooper use their considerable expertise to create new dishes and update old favourites.

Coach and Horses

The quiet and restful Shires Supper Room now provides a standard of cuisine not previously available in Salisbury. The intimate dining room is comfortable, relaxed and informal, and supper is served from 6pm on Mondays to Saturdays.

Alternatively, the Courtyard menu offers an extensive range of home-produced fare from 10am to 10pm every day except Sunday. Visitors also have the option of staying over in one of the two comfortable and well-appointed en suite bedrooms. English Tourist Board 2 crowns commended, the Coach and Horses welcomes children. *Coach and Horses, 39 Winchester Street, Salisbury, Wiltshire Tel: 01722 336254 Fax: 01722 414319*

A good way to find out more about history and layout of Salisbury is to join one of the guided walks which set out from the tourist information centre at the rear of the Guildhall. Walks start at 11am and 6pm each day between late March and early November. For those with a taste for the supernatural, a special ghost walk is available on Friday evenings. Another colourful presentation which offers an insight into the city's past is the thirty-minute Secrets of Salisbury audio-visual guide which is shown in the 13th-century **Medieval Hall** in the Cathedral Close. Each year in late May/early June, the city stages the internationally-renowned Salisbury Festival, a two-week arts extravaganza which offers a wide variety of events, from children's street theatre to orchestral concerts.

Being such a popular visitor centre, Salisbury offers a wide selection of accommodation. For those seeking a peaceful night's rest at a reasonable price, **Farthings** is ideal. This English Tourist Board 2 crown establishment is located in Swayne's Close on the northern side of the city, just seven minutes walk from the Market Square. Proprietor Mrs Gill Rodwell welcomes guests into her comfortable home which enjoys fine views of the cathedral spire and easy parking. An excellent breakfast is served in a charming room which is

Farthings

adorned with an interesting collection of photographs, and there is also a delightful garden where residents can relax and enjoy the tranquil surroundings. A location map is available on request. *Farthings, 9 Swayne's Close, Salisbury, Wiltshire Tel: 01722 330749*

Also located on the northern side of Salisbury between the cathedral and Old Sarum, the **Victoria Lodge Guest House** is a handsome Victorian residence with a very pleasant period feel. Delightfully covered with creeper, this friendly family hotel is conveniently situated for all the amenities of the old city which can be reached via a pleasant riverside walk. The house is comfortable and spacious, and offers fine traditional hospitality and excellent food.

Victoria Lodge Guest House

Most of the neatly presented bedrooms have en suite bathrooms, and all are equipped with colour televisions and hot drinks facilities; there is also a comfortable guest lounge with satellite TV. A generous full English breakfast is served each morning and delicious evening meals are available by arrangement, complimented by a range of wines and spirits from the bar. There is also plenty of safe parking. *Victoria Lodge Guest House, 61 Castle Road, Salisbury, Wiltshire   Tel: 01722 320586 Fax: 01722 414507*

Those looking for bed and breakfast accommodation on the western side of Salisbury should make a point of finding **Websters**, a striking Victorian end-of-terrace property set in a quiet area of the city within easy walking distance of the railway station and centre. The attractive white-painted frontage has an open parking area dotted with large flower-filled tubs, while further splashes of colour are provided by eye-catching hanging baskets and window boxes; a most attractive presentation.

Websters is the home of Mary and Peter Webb, charming hosts who have been providing comfortable accommodation for some years.

The bedrooms are well-appointed and equipped with colour televisions, beverage trays and en suite bathrooms. Of particular interest to disabled guests may be the ground floor twin-bedded room

Websters

whose special facilities have earned a Holiday Care Service Award and a Category 1 listing under the English Tourist Board accessibility scheme. Children over 12 years can be accommodated, as can certain pets by prior arrangement. Supper can also be provided with advance notice. *Websters, 11 Hartington Road, Salisbury, Wiltshire Tel / Fax: 01722 339779*

Outstanding visitor accommodation can also found on the southern side of Salisbury, within easy reach of the centre and the main roads from Bournemouth and Dorchester. The ***Grasmere House Hotel*** is a fine example of a Victorian family residence set in one-and-a-half acres of mature gardens with magnificent towering beech trees and a small woodland fir copse. Built in 1896 for prosperous Salisbury merchants, Grasmere is constructed of deep red brick, with attractive pointed finials on the roof gables.

It has been carefully extended and converted into a delightful private hotel, retaining all the features and atmosphere of a comfortable Victorian home. The conservatory restaurant has spectacular views over Grasmere's lawned garden, and diners will find an imaginative selection of dishes on offer which are prepared using local produce to reflect the seasons. Each guest bedroom has an en suite bathroom, television, telephone, trouser press and hospitality tray, and two are discreetly arranged for disabled guests. The main suite, the Sarisberie, is a conservatory-style room adjacent to the

Grasmere House Hotel

restaurant. Its two rooms can be combined for large private lunches, dinners, dinner-dances and receptions. Grasmere House was the first hotel in Salisbury to be awarded a licence to conduct weddings within the confines of the hotel. AA 3 star and English Tourist Board 3 crowns commended and special short breaks are also available. *Grasmere House Hotel, 70 Harnham Road, Salisbury, Wiltshire Tel: 01722 338388 Fax: 01722 333710*

Britford   *Map 4 ref F10*
1 mile S of Salisbury on the A338
The countryside to the southwest of Salisbury contains some attractive old settlements. The charming hamlet of Britford lies within the branches of the Wiltshire Avon, a couple of miles from the centre of the city. Here, there is a handsome moated country house and a fine **Saxon Church** which predates Salisbury Cathedral by several centuries. The church interior contains some early stone carvings which are believed to date from around 800 AD and three carved door surrounds which were installed before the Norman Conquest.

There is also an unusual, elaborately decorated tomb which is thought to belong to the Duke of Buckingham who was beheaded in

Salisbury in 1483. **Longford Castle** lies to the east of the A338 Fordingbridge road, one mile further south. This largely 16th-century fortification was constructed near the confluence of the Rivers Avon and Ebble to an unusual triangular design; it now houses an interesting collection of paintings.

Nunton   *Map 4 ref F10*
2 miles S of Salisbury on the A338

The lovely old village of Nunton lies close by on the western side of the A338. An attractive community of thatch and brick whose most notable structure is **Nunton House**, it lies in the beautiful valley of the lower Ebble, a river which is said to contain some of the finest trout in the country.

Odstock   *Map 4 ref F10*
2 miles S of Salisbury off the A338

A mile or so upstream, the pleasant riverside community of Odstock possesses a village church which, according to local legend, is subject to an infamous gypsy curse. Its origin surrounds the figure of Joshua Scamp, a notorious local character whose grave lies in the southeast corner of the churchyard. Scamp was a gypsy who in 1801 was wrongfully hanged for stealing horses. This made him a martyr-like figure among the local Romany people and each year on the anniversary of his death, a disorderly crowd would assemble around his grave, usually after having drunk a toast to his memory in the nearby Yew Tree Inn.

One year, the rector resolved to put an end to the unruly gathering, so he locked the door of the church and dug up a wild rose which Scamp's family had planted beside his grave. This action so incensed the gypsy assembly that they placed a curse on anyone who dared to bar them from the church again. Not long after, two men defying the curse met with an untimely end, after which the rector took the key of the church and threw it into the River Ebble where it is said to remain to this day. A briar rose was then re-planted on Scamp's grave which can still be seen beside the crumbling headstone.

Coombe Bissett   *Map 4 ref E10*
3 miles SW of Salisbury on the A354

The charming village of Coombe Bissett lies a couple of miles further upstream at the point where the A354 Salisbury to Blandford Forum road crosses the River Ebble. A rambling country lane to the west of here connects a string of attractive riverside settlements which are sited along the valley of the upper Ebble.

Broad Chalke
Map 3 ref E10
7 miles W of Salisbury off the A354

One of the most westerly of these, Broad Chalke, is the former home of the 17th-century diarist, John Aubrey, whose family owned a small estate in this quiet Saxon village. Aubrey was a warden at the parish church and lived in the Old Rectory. He was also a keen angler and wrote of his beloved River Ebble, *"there are not better trouts in the Kingdom of England than here"*.

Downton
Map 4 ref F11
5 miles S of Salisbury off the A338

Returning to the A338 at the foot of the Ebble valley, the sizable village of Downton lies on the banks of the River Avon, three miles south of its confluence with the Ebble. This ancient settlement was founded by the early Britons who constructed an earthwork fortification above the river. This was later occupied by the Saxons who went on to establish a meeting place or *moot* on the site. This early parliament was commemorated in the 18th century when the present **Moot House** was constructed on the foundations of the old castle.

The building and its garden stand opposite a small 18th-century amphitheatre which was built to resemble the original Saxon meeting place. In 1955, a Roman villa consisting of seven rooms and a bathhouse was discovered near here which is believed to date from around 300 AD. The medieval centre of Downton, with its broad main street and distinctive grassy strip, is known locally as **The Borough**. It was laid out by the Bishop of Winchester in 1205, although most of the thatched brick-built houses which can be seen here today date from the 18th century. The parish church of St Lawrence stands on the site of a Saxon church which is believed to have been consecrated by St Birinus in 638. The present building dates from the 1100s, although it has been much altered over the centuries. Inside, there are some fine carved monuments by the 18th-century Dutch sculptor, Peter Scheemaker. Downton's old manor house is the former home of the Raleigh family and for many years Sir Walter's brother, Carew, was the local Member of Parliament. The large building which can be seen beside the river is a tannery which was first opened in 1918.

Downton also has an exceptionally well-equipped leisure centre with excellent facilities for indoor tennis, cricket, badminton, bowls and five-a-side football. Each Spring Bank Holiday, the village is taken over by the Downton Cuckoo Fair, a traditional event dating back to the 16th century which has much to interest to visitors and locals alike.

Redlynch   *Map 4 ref F11*
6 miles SE of Salisbury off the B3080

Situated a mile and a half along the B3080 New Forest road to the east of Downton, the pleasant community of Redlynch is perhaps best-known for its fine brick-built country mansion, **Newhouse**, which is located a short distance to the northeast of the village. The house has a Jacobean core dating from 1619 and two Georgian wings arranged in the classic trinity configuration. Inside, there is an interesting display of historic costumes, as well as a collection of relics relating to Admiral Nelson.

Lover   *Map 4 ref G11*
6 miles SE of Salisbury off the B3080

The charmingly-named village of Lover lies in the lanes a mile to the southeast of Redlynch. The National Trust-owned **Pepperbox Hill** is situated on the eastern side of the A36, three miles to the northeast of Redlynch. This distinctive knoll is surmounted by an early 17th-century octagonal tower which gives the site its name. One of the earliest follies in Britain, this unique slate-roofed structure enjoys magnificent views over Salisbury and the southeastern corner of Wiltshire. Also known as **Eyre's Folly**, the tower is surrounded by 72 acres of juniper-covered downland which offers some excellent opportunities for walking.

Whiteparish   *Map 4 ref G11*
6 miles SE of Salisbury on the A27

Those looking for accommodation in the southeastern corner of Wiltshire should make a point of finding Whiteparish, an attractive village which is situated at the foot of Pepperbox Hill, on the A27 midway between Salisbury and Romsey. This is the location of **Brickworth Farmhouse**, an 18th-century listed Georgian farmhouse which has been renovated and furnished to retain its period charm. Set in five acres of grounds which incorporate a lovely walled garden, orchard and paddock, the setting is very peaceful and perfect for walking and bird-watching. The decorations in the guest rooms have been carefully chosen, with colourful quilted bedding adding a charming finishing touch.

Hostess Sue Barry is a registered tourist guide who is glad to help her guests plan their excursions. Fresh farm produce and home-baked bread complete the traditional farmhouse experience, and

Brickworth Farmhouse

there are also some excellent local pubs which provide good quality meals at sensible prices. Ideally situated, Brickworth Farmhouse lies within easy reach of Salisbury, the New Forest and the many visitor attractions of southern England. *Brickworth Farmhouse, Brickworth Lane, Whiteparish, Salisbury, Wiltshire   Tel: 01794 884663 Fax: 01794 884581*

Wilton   *Map 4 ref E10*
3 miles W of Salisbury on the A30

On the western side of Salisbury, the ancient market town of Wilton lies near the confluence of the rivers Nadder and Wylye, three miles from the city. The third oldest borough in England, this 2000 year-old settlement was once the capital of Saxon Wessex. In more recent times, it has become internationally renowned for its carpets which continue to be made at the ***Wilton Carpet Factory***, an enterprise which was given a royal charter by William III in 1699.

Carpets are still woven here from local wool using traditional methods, and visitors can join a guided tour which takes in an attractive garden and a museum celebrating 300 years of carpet-making history. (Open daily, 9am to 5pm, all year round.)

The old part of Wilton is centred around the Market Square, a bustling shopping area which contains an interesting collection of early buildings, including the 18th-century town hall and the part-ruined medieval church of St Mary. Market day is Thursday and

Wilton House

with free parking, visitors have access to a wide range of family-owned retailers, pubs, cafes and one of the highest concentrations of antiques shops in Wessex.

Wilton Carpet Factory

Wilton's famous ***Italianate Church*** lies a short walk away, and for those wanting to venture a little further afield, there is an attractive riverside walk along the Wylye which runs from St John's Square through the Flouse Hole conservation area to ***Castle Meadow***, the location of King Stephen's lodge and the site of a bloody Civil War encounter where Maude's troops ambushed and almost captured Charles I when they raided his royal residence.

The magnificent ***Wilton House*** stands on the southeastern edge of Wilton on a site originally occupied by a nunnery founded by Alfred the Great in the 9th century. The nunnery was eventually dissolved by Henry VIII in 1539 and the land given to Sir William Herbert, the future Earl of Pembroke, in whose family it has remained ever since. When the original building was destroyed by fire in 1647, the celebrated architect Inigo Jones was commissioned to build its replacement. He was responsible for designing both the exterior and interior, including and the magnificent single and double cube state rooms. The house was further remodelled at the beginning of the 19th century by James Wyatt, who designed the present north and west fronts and the Gothic-style cloisters. Today, Wilton House contains an outstanding collection of art, including paintings by Rembrandt, Van Dyke, Rubens and Tintoretto, and furniture by Chippendale and Kent.

There are also famous collections of model soldiers and miniature teddy bears, a magnificent Tudor kitchen, and a Victorian laundry. The 21-acre grounds are also well worth investigating. Originally laid out by Isaac de Caus, they are known for their distinctive cedar trees, Roger Morris' elegant Palladian bridge of 1737, and Sir William Chambers' casino. During World War II, Wilton House was used as an operations centre for southern command and the Normandy landings are believed to have been planned here. (Open daily, 11am to 6pm between late March and early November.)

Netherhampton   *Map 4 ref E10*
2 miles W of Salisbury on the A3094

The ***Victoria and Albert*** is a charming 16th-century inn and restaurant which is situated to the southeast of Wilton in the attractive village of Netherhampton. Run by Sarah and Nigel Allen, this quintessentially English village pub has a thatched roof, exposed beams and an abundance of genuine character. Along with a wide selection of locally-brewed real ales, a comprehensive range of dishes

Victoria and Albert

is served, with the steak and ale pie and vegetarian choices being strongly recommended. With its quarter-acre garden, there is plenty of room for the whole family to unwind, drink and dine al fresco in fine weather. The Victoria and Albert lies within an area renowned for its golfing, racing and country walks, making this the ideal place to relax and enjoy fine food, drink and hospitality. *Victoria and Albert, Netherhampton, Near Salisbury, Wiltshire Tel: 01722 743174*

Salisbury Racecourse *Map 4 ref E10*
3 miles W of Salisbury off the A354
The famous Salisbury Racecourse is situated midway between Netherhampton and Coombe Bissett, two miles across the downs to the south. One of the oldest courses in England, horses have raced on this scenic downland site since the 16th century. Meetings are held during the summer months, combining high quality flat racing with an enjoyable day out; accompanied children under 16 are welcome and admitted free.

Fovant *Map 3 ref D10*
8 miles W of Salisbury on the A30
The distinctive **Fovant Hill Regimental Badges** are located beside the A30, five miles to the west of Wilton. Easily viewed from a lay-by on the main road, these giant outlines were carved into the side of the chalk escarpment by soldiers stationed at the nearby training camp during the First World War. Their upkeep is funded by voluntary subscriptions from all over the world.

Dinton *Map 3 ref D10*
9 miles W of Salisbury off the A30
Two attractive National Trust properties are located a couple of miles to the north of Fovant village near the lovely hillside community of Dinton. The first, **Little Clarendon**, is a small yet impressive early-Tudor manor house which was extensively altered in the 17th century. It is located a quarter of a mile to the east of Dinton church and is open to the public by prior appointment only (telephone 01985 843600). The second, **Philipps House**, is a handsome white-fronted neo-Grecian residence which situated to the west of the village. Designed in the early 19th century by the architect Jeffry Wyattville, it stands within the beautiful landscaped grounds of Dinton Park.

The house has recently undergone a major programme of restoration; however, the 120-acre park remains open throughout the year. Dinton village also contains the 17th-century **Lawes Cottage** which was the home of the composer and associate of John Milton, William Lawes. Part of his score for Milton's Masque of Comus is thought to have been written here in 1634.

Wylye
Map 3 ref D9

10 miles NW of Salisbury on the A36

A minor road to the north of Dinton leads across the downs to the peaceful village of Wylye, a long-established settlement which was once an important junction and staging post on the main London to Exeter coaching route. At one time, the village could boast nine inns; today, however, it is bypassed by the A303 and A36 and only the 14th-century Bell Inn remains. A statue near the bridge over the River Wylye (from which Wilton and Wiltshire also get their names) commemorates a brave but unfortunate post-boy who drowned here after rescuing several passengers from a stagecoach which had overturned during a flood.

The A303 to the northeast of Wylye passes beneath the spectacular but little-visited Iron Age hill fort of **Yarnbury Castle**. Dating from the 2nd century BC, this striking series of grassy ramparts encloses a 28-acre hilltop which affords some spectacular views over the southern fringe of Salisbury Plain. The Iron Age banks and ditches, which seem a haven of tranquillity compared to the clamour of Stonehenge, are set around an earthwork fortification dating from an earlier period.

Winterbourne Stoke
Map 4 ref E8

8 miles NW of Salisbury on the A303

The attractive village of Winterbourne Stoke can easily be missed, being tucked away down a cul-de-sac off the A303, two and a half miles to the east of Yarnbury Castle. However, its pretty stone cottages, 13th-century church and flint and stone-fronted manor house are well worth a detour. A series of about twenty Neolithic burial mounds, or barrows, can be found on the eastern side of the village. Most are thought to have been constructed by the Beaker people who migrated here from continental Europe around 2500 BC.

Berwick St James
Map 4 ref E9

7 miles NW of Salisbury on the B3083

To the south of Winterbourne Stoke, the B3083 leads through the village to Berwick St James to its junction with the A36 near Stapleford, the site of a castle which belonged to William the Conqueror's chief huntsman, Waleran. The early Norman village church contains some impressive banded columns which are typical of the period. The etched grid of the medieval board game, **Nine Men's Morris**, can just be made out on the stone bench in the church porch. The minor road running along opposite bank of the River Wylye to

Stapleford connects some delightful unspoilt villages. These include Little, Steeple and Hanging Langford, settlements characterised by their chequered flint houses and thatched brick cottages.

Great Wishford
Map 4 ref E9

5 miles NW of Salisbury on the A36

A little further downstream, the larger community of Great Wishford possesses some fine 17th-century almshouses, a rare 18th-century fire engine, and an unusual sign on the churchyard wall which records the price of bread at various points during the last 200 years. For example, in 1800 the cost of a gallon of bread dough was 3s 4d, in 1904 it was only 10d, and in 1924 it was 2s 8d. Each year on Oak Apple Day, 29th May, the citizens of Great Wishford celebrate their ancient right to cut and gather timber in nearby *Grovely Wood* by marching onto the wooded ridge and returning with freshly cut branches. Later in the day, a party from the village dances on Salisbury's cathedral green carrying bundles of sticks known as *nitches*.

Old Sarum
Map 4 ref F9

2 miles N of Salisbury off the A345

Old Sarum, the original site of Salisbury, lies on a windswept hillside two miles to the north of the present city centre. This ancient stronghold, which can be found on the western side of the A345 Amesbury road, was successively an Iron Age hill fort, a Roman settlement known as Sorviodunum, and a bustling medieval cathedral town. The Saxons named it Searobyrg meaning *"dry place"*, and this reference to a lack of water may be another reason why the bishops decided to move their cathedral to another more hospitable site in the 13th century. Today, this dramatic hilltop is uninhabited, and all that remains of the once-glorious 56-acre fortifications are some ruined fragments of the castle walls and an outline of the foundations of the original cathedral and bishop's palace. However, the massive conical earthwork is still highly impressive and is well worth a visit.

Now under the guardianship of English Heritage, it is open daily, 10am to 6pm, all year round. Despite having an electorate which at one time numbered only ten, Old Sarum returned two MPs to Westminster before the 1832 Reform Act put an end to the so-called *"rotten boroughs"*. A plaque on the site commemorates the constituency's most illustrious MP, the 18th-century orator and statesman William Pitt the Elder. Nearby Old Sarum Flying Club offers breathtaking flights over the Wiltshire countryside.

Stratford-sub-Castle
Map 4 ref F10

1 mile NW of Salisbury off the A345

Below Old Sarum lies Stratford-sub-Castle, a tranquil community of 17th and 18th-century houses lying on the banks of the River Avon. Another impressive Iron Age hill fort lies beside the A30 Stockbridge road, three miles to the east of Old Sarum. Now under the ownership of the National Trust, **Figsbury Ring** enjoys some excellent views over Salisbury and the Avon Valley.

The area of chalk downland between the A30 and A338 to the northeast of Figsbury Ring forms part of the top secret military establishment, **Porton Down**. Except on rare occasions, this bleak upland has been barred to the public for over fifty years. Ironically, this has led to it becoming a unique conservation area which is home a wide variety of rare plants, flowers and birds. Indeed, the great bustard has successfully been reintroduced here following its local eradication in the early 19th century. This large long-legged bird, which is featured on Wiltshire's coat of arms, was once a common sight on Salisbury Plain before before it was wiped out by over-enthusiastic riflemen. Old Sarum's hilltop site rises about the beautiful unspoilt valley of the Wiltshire Avon.

Woodford Valley
Map 4 ref F9

6 miles N of Salisbury off the A345

Known locally as the Woodford Valley, the seven-mile stretch between Salisbury and Amesbury contains some of the loveliest and most peaceful villages in Wiltshire, including **Great Durnford** with its Norman church, restored mill and picturesque cricket pitch, **Lake** with its impressive Tudor mansion, and **Middle Woodford**, home of an internationally-renowned garden. The beautifully landscaped **Heale Garden and Plant Centre** lies within the eight-acre grounds of Heale House, an elegant mansion dating from the late 16th century which stands in an idyllic position beside the Avon. Much of the house remains unaltered since Charles II took refuge here following the Battle of Worcester in 1651. The garden's superb collection of plants, shrubs and roses, many of which are on sale in the plant centre, are grown in a variety of formal and informal settings, and the grounds contain some fine mellow stonework, a water garden, a Japanese teahouse, and the elegant Nikko Bridge. (Open daily, 10am to 5pm, all year round.)

Amesbury
Map 4 ref F8

8 miles N of Salisbury on the A345

Two winding country lanes, one on the east bank, one on the west, follow the bends in the river, which along this stretch is shallow, wide and fairly fast-flowing. A bridge connects the villages of **Netton** and **Upper Woodford**, and from here it is a four-mile drive along the west bank of the Avon to the ancient monastic town of Amesbury. According to Mallory, Queen Guinevere withdrew to a nunnery at Amesbury on hearing of King Arthur's death. However, a more verifiable account records that Queen Elfrida founded an abbey here around 979 in reparation for her part in the murder of her son-in-law, Edward the Martyr, at Corfe Castle. Almost two centuries later, Henry II rebuilt the abbey's great church of St Mary and St Melor in a cruciform shape with a tall central tower. Sadly, this is the only structure to survive from the pre-Norman monastery, the present-day **Amesbury Abbey** being a large Victorian mansion which operates as a private nursing home. It is not open to the public, although its gardens occasionally are.

A pleasant shopping town set around a bend in the river, Amesbury is connected to its sister settlement of **West Amesbury** by the graceful five-arched Palladian-style **Queensbury Bridge**. Some exceptional historic features are to be found on the west side of the Avon, including the site of an ancient earthwork, Vespasian's Camp, and the 17th-century West Amesbury House. The rows of 100 year-old beech trees standing beside the A303 to the west of the town are said to represent the ranks of English and French ships at the Battle of the Nile.

Woodhenge   *Map 4 ref F8*
9 miles N of Salisbury off the A345

A mile to the north of Amesbury, the A345 Marlborough road passes along the eastern side of Woodhenge, an ancient ceremonial monument which predates Stonehenge by several hundred years. This is one of the first historic sites in Britain to have been discovered by aerial photography, its six concentric rings of post holes having been spotted as cropmarks by Squadron-Leader Insall in 1925. Believed to date from the late Neolithic period around 2200 BC, the site consisted of a series of timber uprights which are now indicated by concrete posts.

Like nearby Stonehenge, these were positioned to predict the sun's path across the sky on Midsummer's Day and served as an astronomical calendar. The one and a half acre site was extensively excavated in the late 1920s and a number of Neolithic artefacts were discovered, including flint scrapers, arrow heads and two ceremonial chalk axes. Perhaps the most striking find, however, was unearthed in the centre of the circle: the skeleton of a three year-old

Stonehenge

child with a fractured skull who could well have been the victim of a ritual sacrifice.

The whole area is surrounded by a circular ditch some 220ft in diameter which is bordered to the northeast by another Neolithic structure, **Durrington Walls**. This once-spectacular earthwork enclosed an 80ft ditch and is now bisected by the Amesbury to Marlborough road. The two sites probably formed a single religious observatory which, for some unknown reason, was abandoned around 1800 BC.

Cholderton

To the north and east of Woodhenge, the landscape is somewhat marred by rows of uniform military housing. The **Cholderton Rare Breeds Farm** is situated near the junction of the A303 and A338, four miles to the east of Amesbury. This interesting establishment specialises in centuries-old breeds of domestic animals, including pigs, sheep, cattle and over fifty breeds of rabbit. A selection of baby animals can be seen during the spring and summer months, and amusing pig races are held at peak times. The farm offers trailer rides, and incorporates a nature trail, water garden, adventure playground, picnic area, cafe and shop. (Open daily, 10am to 6pm between late March and late October.)

Stonehenge

a World Heritage Site and one of the most famous megalithic monuments in Europe, stands on an gently-sloping hillside, two and a half miles to the west of Woodhenge. Crowded by the nearby A303 east-west trunk road and appearing strangely dwarfed by the open expanse of Salisbury Plain, it is not until it is approached on foot through the tunnel under the A360 that the true scale of this spectacular Bronze Age monument becomes clear. In fact, some of its great stone blocks stand over twenty feet high and are embedded up to eight feet in the ground. The most central area consists of an inner horseshoe and an outer ring of massive sarsen (meaning *foreign*) stones with equally massive lintels which were brought all the way from the Marlborough Downs, twenty miles away to the north.

This inner formation is surrounded by a double outer circle of eighty standing stones which were erected many years previously. Incredibly, these rare *"bluestones"* originated in the Preseli Hills of west Wales and had to be transported over 200 miles to Salisbury Plain. The largest bluestone, the Altar Stone, stands at the very centre of the monument and the rising sun, when viewed from here on the longest day of the year, can be seen to appear over the smaller

Heel Stone, some 256ft away to the northeast. The entire Stonehenge site, which incorporates earthworks, burial mounds and other henge monuments, is thought to be part of a gigantic astronomical calendar which was constructed over many centuries for the purpose of observing ancient sun-worshipping rituals. The visitor area incorporates a cafe and gift shop and is open daily, 9am to 7pm (earlier in winter) all year round.

CHAPTER TWO
Westbury to the Dorset Border

Old Wardour Castle

2

Westbury to the Dorset Border

Warminster

Map 1 ref C8

4 miles S of Westbury on the A350

Warminster, the largest centre of population in the eastern section of south Wiltshire, is a historic wool and coaching town which contains some handsome 18th and 19th-century buildings, including three fine old coaching inns. Its famous school, which was founded in 1707, contains a doorway designed by Christopher Wren which was originally installed at Longleat House. Conversely, the organ in the impressive 14th-century minster church was originally intended for Salisbury cathedral. To the west of Warminster, the land rises onto the 800ft *Cley Hill*, part of the ancient Ridgeway which once ran all the way from South Devon to the Wash. Nearby *Warminster Common* offers some pleasant woodland walking and fine views.

Westbury

Map 1 ref C7

24 miles NW of Salisbury on the A350

The small market town of Westbury lies four miles to the north of Warminster at the junction of the A350 and A3098; it is also a well-known railway junction on the main Paddington to Penzance line. The town contains an imposing town hall, some fine Georgian houses and a pleasant little market place.

Situated a mile to the southwest of Westbury town centre, the impressive *Hollies Inn* can be found on the A3098 Westbury to Frome road at Westbury Leigh. This handsome redbrick coaching inn dates back to the 1620s and is full of genuine character and charm. It has been run as a family concern since 1991 by Steve, Lyn and Phil and is known throughout the area for its excellent food.

The incredibly varied menu features one of the largest steak and kidney pies one is ever likely to see, or if the taste buds long for something more exotic, there are such specialities as kangaroo, ostrich or emu steaks, served with one of the inn's delicious homemade sauces. All dishes are prepared using the freshest local ingredients and there is seating for up to sixty people.

Hollies Inn

For those partaking in a little too much good food and wine, the inn also offers comfortable bed and breakfast accommodation in six en suite guest rooms. The Hollies Inn lies within a mile of the National Cycle Route and is truly a haven of refreshment and hospitality. *Hollies Inn, 55 Westbury Leigh, Westbury, Wiltshire Tel: 01373 864493*

Westbury is perhaps best-known for its distinctive **White Horse** which can be seen on the side of the 755ft Westbury Hill, two miles to the east of the town. Reputed to be the oldest of Wiltshire's eleven hill figures, it was carved into the chalk hillside to commemorate King Alfred's defeat of the Danes on nearby Tenantry Down in 878 AD, then was subsequently restored in the 18th century. The head of the horse stands below the ramparts of **Bratton Castle**, a spectacularly-sited Iron Age hill fort covering 25 acres which can be reached via Bratton village. Those climbing to the top will be rewarded with outstanding views over the surrounding countryside.

Brokerswood
Map 1 ref B7

3 miles NW of Westbury off the A36

The times are long gone since the days of help-yourself service with a biscuit tin set on top of the beer barrels for customers to put their money in, but such were the beginnings of the Kicking Donkey at Brokerswood.

Situated in delightful countryside to the north of Westbury Leigh, the inn was known in the 1800s as the Yew Tree when it was literally the owner's front parlour, with sweet jars on the windowsill and the beer cellar in the back room.

Kicking Donkey

Today, the Kicking Donkey is a very popular country pub which has recently been included in the Good Beer Guide 1997 and Trencherman's Guide to the best pubs and inns in the south. An attractive inn with rustic surrounds and a large garden, it offers a wide selection meals, both in the dining room and the front bar, where lighter meals and daily specials are regularly available. As with all meals, the Sunday roast offers excellent value for money.

The Kicking Donkey has good facilities for children and disabled customers, and lies within easy reach of Rode Bird Gardens, Longleat and the Westbury White Horse, with Bath only twenty minutes away. *Kicking Donkey, Brokerswood, Near Westbury, Wiltshire Tel: 01373 823250*

Edington
Map 1 ref C7
3 miles E of Westbury on the B3098

The tiny community of Edington lies just to the north of the B3098 Market Lavington road, one mile east of Bratton. Despite its present size, the village was once a place of some importance and indeed, its 14th-century church seems to have been built to almost cathedral-like proportions. During a rebellion against Henry VI's corrupt government in 1450, the Bishop of Salisbury was dragged from his residence here and stoned to death on top of nearby Golden Hall Hill.

Heytesbury
Map 3 ref C8
6 miles SE of Westburyon the A36

A number of attractive settlements lie along the valley of the River Wylye to the southeast of Warminster. The sizable village of Heytesbury lies beside the A36, close to its junction with the B390. During Norman times, this was an important ecclesiastical centre and the parish **Church of St Peter and St Paul** was a collegiate institution with its own dean and chapter of canons. Much of this fine cruciform structure dates from the 13th century, though like many of its rural counterparts throughout Wessex, it was extensively remodelled during the Victorian era. On this occasion, however, the restoration was carried out under the careful supervision of architect William Butterfield who preserved many of the existing medieval features, including the fine fan vaulting and intricate stone screen in the north transept.

The building known as the **Hospital of St John** is an almshouse which was founded in the 15th century by the Hungerford family. The present structure is a Georgian replacement which was erected after the original burnt down in the mid 18th century.

Imber
Map 1 ref D7
5 miles E of Westbury off the B3098

One of the strangest villages in Wiltshire lies within the Salisbury Plain Military Training Area to the north of Heytesbury. The ghost-village of Imber remains permanently out of bounds, except on one or two occasions each year when the Ministry of Defence grants special permission for the public to enter. In 1943, the population was evicted by the army on the understanding they would be allowed to return to their homes when the Second World War was over. However, the MoD failed to keep its promise and the villagers remain in exile to this day. All that remains of their community is the shell of the village church and a collection of decaying cottages, many of which have been given concrete frontages to provide more suitable conditions for training soldiers in modern street fighting. Each year in September, a service is held in the church to commemorate this curious lost community.

Corton
Map 3 ref C8

6 miles SE of Westbury off the A36

The tranquil community of Corton lies in the heart of the upper Wylye valley, a mile and a half to the south of Heytesbury. Easily reached from the A36 at Upton Lovell, the village is well worth visiting for its delightful 18th-century inn, **The Dove**. This handsome traditional pub and eating place is owned and personally-run by William Gough, a friendly host who takes pride in having up to five real cask beers available at any one time.

Dove Inn

The bar area is relaxed and welcoming, and benefits from a warming open fire during the winter months. The restaurant seats up to 35 people and offers a wide range of dishes, from light snacks to full meals. The Sunday roasts are locally renowned and are served throughout the year except in the height of summer. At that time of the year, the spacious gardens prove very popular with visitors, who gather to enjoy a glass of beer or eat al fresco. The Dove Inn is a must for all those who enjoy good food, fine ale and warm traditional hospitality. *Dove Inn, Corton, Near Warminster, Wiltshire Tel: 01985 850109*

Longleat House

Codford St Peter, Codford St Mary   Map 3 ref D8
8 miles SE of Westbury on the A36

The sister villages of Codford St Peter and Codford St Mary are situated on the northern side of the A36, two miles to the east of Corton. The communities lie beneath the prehistoric remains of **Codford Circle**, an ancient hilltop meeting place which stands 617ft up on Salisbury Plain. The church in Codford St Peter contains an exceptional Saxon stone carving which is thought to date from the 9th century. Reputed to be part of a stone cross, it portrays a man holding a branch who is engaged in some kind of ritual dance. An unexpectedly powerful piece, it is widely regarded as one of Wiltshire's finest treasures.

Stockton   Map 3 ref D9
9 miles SE of Westbury on the A36

The tranquil community of Stockton lies on the southern side of the upper Wylye, a mile to the southeast of Codford St Mary. **Stockton House**, a handsome residence with mullioned windows and banded flint stonework, was built by an Elizabethan merchant named Topp. Topp was also responsible for constructing the elegant almshouses which are set around three sides of a square courtyard a short distance away.

Longleat   Map 3 ref B8
6 miles SW of Westbury off the A362

Moving round to the western side of Warminster, perhaps the most famous stately home in England lies four miles from the town off the A362 Frome road. **Longleat House** is a magnificent Elizabethan mansion which was designed by Robert Smythson for Sir John Thynne, an ancestor of the present owners, the Marquess and Marchioness of Bath. Built to a largely symmetrical design, the imposing three-storey building was begun in 1568 and was still under construction at the time of Thynne's death in 1580.

Over the centuries, the interior has been furnished with some superb works of art, including tapestries, period furniture, velvet and leather work, and paintings by old masters such as Titian and Reynolds. Among the many interesting attractions to be seen at the house are the waistcoat worn by Charles I at the time of this execution, the official robes of the Baths, the atmospheric Victorian kitchen, and the state coach.

One of Longleat's more unusual occupants is the ghostly Green Lady who is said to wander the top-floor corridors. She is rumoured to be the spirit of Louisa Carteret whose husband, Thomas Thynne, the second Viscount Weymouth, is alleged to have killed her lover in a duel. The Viscount then concealed the body in the cellar where it remained undisturbed until the early 20th century when it was accidentally discovered under the flagstones.

The magnificent grounds of Longleat House were landscaped by Capability Brown and now contain one of the best-known safari parks in the country. The famous **Lions of Longleat**, which were first introduced in 1966, have been followed by a number of other exotic animals, including elephants, rhinos, zebras and white tigers. The park also features safari boat rides, a narrow gauge railway, children's amusement area, garden centre and one of the largest mazes in the world. It can also be very crowded, particularly on summer weekends. (House open daily, 10am to 6pm, all year round; safari park open daily, 10am to 5.30pm between mid March and early November.)

Horningsham   Map 3 ref B8
6 miles SW of Westbury off the A362
The ancient village of Horningsham lies on the southern edge of the Longleat estate and can be reached along a lane from the A362 or B3092. The settlement's name is reputed to mean *"bastard's farm"* from the Saxon words *"horning"*, meaning bastard, and *"ham"*, meaning farm. The village is referred to in the Domesday Book of 1086, and there is also evidence of even earlier occupation by the Romans.

Present-day Horningsham contains some fine old buildings, including the part-medieval **St John the Baptist's church**, a row of 14th to 16th-century thatched almshouses, the 18th-century Bath Arms inn, and the historic Old Meeting Place which was built in 1568 as a place of worship by the Presbyterian masons who were brought down from Scotland to work at Longleat House.

Stourton   Map 3 ref B9
9 miles SW of Westbury off the B3092
The beautiful National Trust-owned estate village of Stourton lies five miles to the south of Horningsham along the B3092 Mere road. A neat community of estate cottages with a pub and a tiny post office, it lies at the bottom of a steep wooded valley and is especially pretty during the daffodil season and in early-summer.

Stourton's main attraction, however, is the adjoining **Stourhead Estate**, a jewel in the crown of the National Trust which incorporates one of the most remarkable landscaped gardens in Europe.

Visitors are encouraged to leave their cars in the large car park on the ridge above the village and proceed on foot. The main part of **Stourhead House** was built between 1721 and 1724, the library and picture gallery having been added a few years later. It was designed in Palladian style by the architect Colen Campbell for a wealthy Bristol banker and is one of the first examples of a Georgian country mansion in the United Kingdom.

The house contains some superb works of art, including furniture by Chippendale the Younger, intricate woodcarving by Grinling Gibbons and a collection of paintings and sculpture by such artists as Angelica Kauffman and Michael Rysbrack. (House open daily, except Thursdays and Fridays, 12 noon to 5.30pm between late March and early November.)

Stourhead House

It was the original owner's son, however, who made the biggest impression on the Stourhead estate. Between 1741 and 1780, Henry Hoare II designed and laid out one of the most outstanding landscaped gardens of his day. Using a broad range of classical and contemporary influences, he created a superb *"18th-century Disneyland"* which is peppered with elegant features, including a 14th-century High Cross brought from Bristol in 1765, a graceful arched stone bridge by the lake, a neo-Roman pantheon, and an exquisite white-painted stone rotunda known as the Temple of the Sun.

The gardens are renowned for their striking vistas and woodland walks, and are planted with a stunning selection of rare trees

Stourhead Monument

and specimen shrubs, including tulip trees, azaleas and rhododen-drons. In 1946, the Hoare family presented Stourhead to the National Trust who have continued the process of introducing unusual plant varieties. (Gardens open daily, 8am to 7pm, or dusk if earlier, all year round.)

The impressive **King Alfred's Tower** stands at the summit of the 790ft Kingsettle Hill on the northwestern edge of the Stourhead estate. This 160ft triangular redbrick folly was built in 1772 in commemoration of the great King of Wessex who is reputed to have raised his standard against the Danes at this point in 878. Those climbing to the top are rewarded with a glorious view which takes in the three counties of Wiltshire, Dorset and Somerset. The tower lies three and a half miles by road from Stourhead House and is open daily, except Fridays and non-Bank Holiday Mondays, 2pm to 5.30pm between late March and early November.)

Mere   *Map 3 ref B10*
10 miles SW of Westbury off the A303

The National Trust also owns **Whitesheet Hill**, the site of an Iron Age hill fort which lies on the Stourhead estate some distance to the northeast of the main gardens. Thankfully now bypassed by the A303 east-west trunk route, the attractive small town of Mere lies on the western edge of Salisbury Plain, two and a half miles to the southeast of Stourhead. This historic community takes its name from the merchant adventurer, John Mere, who founded a chantry here in the 14th century. Dating from three centuries earlier, the handsome former chantry church of St Michael has a fine Perpendicular tower, one of the pinnacles of which has been struck by lightning three times in the last hundred years alone, contradicting the old saying that lightning never strikes in the same place twice. The church contains some fine medieval glass, an unusual octagonal font and two monumental brasses dating from the turn of the 15th century.

The Dorset dialect poet, William Barnes, lived adjacent to the church in the handsome 15th-century residence known as the Old Chantry. He also ran his own school in a room above the **Old Market Hall** in the town square. The Victorian clock tower which can be seen nearby was gifted to the townspeople by the Prince of Wales in 1868. Mere also possesses two lovely old coaching inns, the Old Ship, with its 18th-century wrought-iron sign commemorating the family crest of John Mere, and the Talbot, which is reputed to have given shelter to Charles II following the Royalist defeat at the Battle of Worcester in 1651. (According to local legend, the King then went on to stay at Zeals House a couple of miles to the west.)

The countryside around Mere contains some interesting places to visit, including the **White Sheet Nature Reserve**, which is known for its rare chalk-loving butterflies, and the medieval field system known as **The Lynchets,** Mere, which has recently been opened up to visitors the Countryside Commission. Magnificent views over the Blackmoor Vale can be enjoyed from the top of nearby **Castle Hill**, the site of a now-demolished fortification built by Richard, Earl of Cornwall.

Shaftesbury
Map 3 ref C11
18 miles S of Westbury on the A350

The lovely Dorset border town of Shaftesbury stands at the busy junction of the A30 and A350 east-west/north-south routes. Referred to as *"Shaston"* in the novels of Thomas Hardy, the town is perhaps best known for its steep medieval cobbled lane, **Gold Hill**, a unique curved thoroughfare which is lined with old cottages on one side and a massive buttressed wall on the other. In recent decades it has been much photographed and filmed, one of its most prominent appearances being in a long-running television commercial for brown bread. The stiff climb to the 700ft summit of Gold Hill is rewarded some glorious views over the surrounding landscape.

King Alfred founded an abbey for nuns in Shaftesbury around 888 AD and installed his daughter Aethelgifa as the first abbess. Then in 978, the fifteen year-old Anglo-Saxon King Edward the Martyr was buried here following his murder at Corfe Castle. His tomb became an important place of pilgrimage and during the medieval period, Shaftesbury grew as a centre of commerce and religion. The abbey was finally abandoned in 1539 as part of Henry VIII's Dissolution of the Monasteries; shortly before, however, the abbess is rumoured to have secreted the abbey's considerable hoard of treasure somewhere in the town. The cache has never been found, and according to local legend, the only one to know its hiding place is the ghost of a monk who is occasionally seen walking in the old abbey grounds.

Ashmore
Map 3 ref C11
4 miles SE of Shaftesbury off the B3081

The charming village of Ashmore lies off the B3081 Tollard Royal road, five miles to the southeast of Shaftesbury. Standing at over 700ft above sea level on the steep wooded ridge of chalk downland known as **Cranborne Chase**, this is one of the highest settlements in the area. All the more remarkable, then, that it should possess an enormous village pond, some 120ft in diameter and 16ft deep at its centre. The settlement is recorded in the Domesday Book as *"Aisemare"*, meaning pool by the ash tree, and its unlikely supply of water has never been known to dry up, even in the most severe drought. Each year at midsummer, the present-day villagers continue to celebrate its existence in the ancient ceremony of *"Filly Loo"*: a platform is set up in the centre of the pond, upon which a band plays whilst teams of Morris dancers from all over the region dance around the edge.

Tollard Royal   Map 3 ref C11
6 miles SE of Shaftesbury on the B3081

Set in the heart of Cranborne Chase, the historic village of Tollard Royal stands at the top of Zigzag Hill, two miles to the east of Ashmore. The community's royal association dates back to King John, who owned a small estate here and often hunted on the surrounding land which at that time was densely wooded. A reminder of this once-great primeval forest is the fragmented belt of woodland known as the **Inner Chase** which covers the downland ridge to the east and west of the village. The local connection with the medieval king is reflected in the name of the village inn and in King John's House, an impressive part stone, part timber-framed residence dating from the 13th century which once served as the royal hunting lodge. The building's immaculate present-day condition is largely due to the efforts of General Pitt Rivers, an obsessive Victorian archeologist who, after inheriting the estate, spent the last two decades of his life unearthing its many Bronze Age remains. The general founded a museum in the nearby village of Farnham to display his extensive collection of historic artefacts; however, this was closed in the 1960s and its exhibits transferred to **Oxford and the South Wiltshire Museum** in Salisbury which has a gallery named after him.

Tollard Royal's late 13th-century village church is dedicated, somewhat unusually, to St Peter Ad Vincula (St Peter in chains). The building contains the tomb of General Pitt Rivers and stands within a delightful churchyard near the village centre. The general was also responsible for laying out the nearby **Larmer Tree Victorian Pleasure Gardens**, the original *"larmer tree"* being the ancient meeting place where King John used to rendezvous with his hunting party. Originally opened in 1880, the gardens were intended for *"the recreation of the people of the neighbouring towns and villages"*. They contain a wonderful assortment of exotic features, in-

The Great Portal Entrance to the Main Hall
Wardour Castle

cluding Indian-style buildings, a Roman temple and an amphitheatre, all set within superb tree-filled grounds inhabited by ornamental pheasants, peacocks and free-flying macaws.

Open-air concerts are presented on summer Sundays, and there is also a croquet lawn, a refreshment terrace and a plant sales area. Larmer Gardens continue to be owned and run by the general's great-grandson, Michael Pitt Rivers , and are open on Sundays, Thursdays and Bank Holiday Mondays (also Tuesdays and Wednesdays in July and August), 11am to 6pm between late April and late September.

Ludwell   Map 3 ref C11
2 miles E of Shaftesbury on the A30

The minor road which connects with the B3081 Tollard Royal to Shaftesbury road to the A30 at Ludwell runs along the western edge of the National Trust-owned **Win Green Hill**, the highest point in Cranborne Chase and indeed in Wiltshire. The hill is crowned by a copse of beech trees set around an ancient bowl barrow and from the top, there are wonderful views as far as the Quantock Hills to the northwest and the Isle of Wight to the southeast.

Berwick St John   Map 3 ref C11
3 miles E of Shaftesbury off the A30

The attractive community of Berwick St John lies at the head of the valley of the River Ebble, three miles to the north of Tollard Royal as the crow flies, although somewhat further by road. The village is encircled by high downland and according to local legend, it is possible to summon the Devil by cursing at the top of one's voice while walking seven times round **Winkelbury Camp**, the Iron Age hill fort which lies to the north of the village. When called in this manner, Satan is said to appear riding a black horse and will grant his summoner a single wish. The risk of an unwelcome appearance by the Devil may be at the root of one of Berwick St John's less unnerving customs. Thanks to a legacy left by the vicar for this purpose, the church bells were tolled for ten minutes at eight o'clock each evening to direct travellers lost on the downs to safety, a tradition which lasted for over 200 years between the mid 18th century and the Second World War.

Ansty   Map 3 ref D10
5 miles E of Shaftesbury off A30

Lying to the north of Winkelbury Camp Iron Age hill fort and just off the A30 Shaftesbury to Wilton road, the peaceful village of Ansty is the entry point to **Old Wardour Castle**, a ruined 14th-century fortification which is signposted from the village along a long winding lane. In 1643, the 61 year-old Lady Arundel and a garrison of fifty Royalist guards held the castle for six days against a 1300-strong Parliamentarian force. The indomitable lady is believed to have agreed to surrender only after being offered acceptable terms; terms which were immediately disregarded by Cromwell's troops. Instead, Lady Arundel was thrown into the castle dungeons from where she is thought to have escaped through a secret passage, probably a castle drain.

Old Wardour Castle

To avenge the Parliamentarian double-dealing, her son returned to besiege the castle, and the combined effects of the two bombardments led to its eventual abandonment. Present-day visitors can view the substantial remains of Old Wardour Castle with its unique hexagonal courtyard, beautiful lake and unusual rockwork grotto close by.

This tranquil site is an ideal location for walking and picnicking, and is open daily, 10am to 6pm, all year round (closed Mondays and Tuesdays in winter). The old castle stands within the extensive wooded grounds of *new* Wardour Castle, an 18th-century Palladian mansion which is now a girls' school and not open to the public. An exceptionally fine baroque chapel adjoins the school whose striking interior contains some impressive works of art.

Tisbury
Map 3 ref C10

5 miles NE of Shaftesbury off the A30

An undulating lane to the north of Ansty descends into the beautiful valley of the upper Nadder. After crossing the main railway line at the foot of the hill, the road arrives in Tisbury, an attractive community which contains what is believed to be the largest surviving tithe barn in England. These colossal buildings were constructed to store *"tithes"*, one tenth of the local tenant farmers' annual crops which were payable to the owners of church lands. The magnificent barn at Tisbury stands on the site of **Place Farm**, part of a medieval estate which belonged to the Abbess of Shaftesbury. Built of stone in the 15th century, the 190ft long structure has thirteen pairs of storage bays and a thatched roof which encloses around a third of an acre. A complex assembly of beams and timber uprights, its interior has an almost cathedral-like quality. Much of the medieval farmyard has also survived, including its impressive 14th-century double gatehouse.

Elsewhere in Tisbury, the 13th-century **Church of St John the Baptist** has a splendid carved roof and a tower which supported a tall spire until the latter collapsed in 1762. Its striking pulpit, pews and font cover all date from the 17th century. **Pyt House**, an elegant Palladian-style Georgian country residence, can be found in the lanes, two and a half miles west of the village. This was the scene of a notorious confrontation between angry farm workers and mounted soldiers during the agricultural protests of 1830. (Open Wednesdays and Thursdays, 2.30pm to 5pm between May and September.)

Chilmark
Map 3 ref D9

7 miles NE of Shaftesbury on the B3089

A number of interesting communities lie on the ridge above the River Nadder to the northeast of Tisbury. Chilmark is the site of a celebrated quarry from which the material for Salisbury Cathedral, Wilton House and many other fine buildings in the area was taken. Stone was first quarried here by the Romans, and several centuries of workings have left a network of deep tunnels and vaults which are now used by the Ministry of Defence for storing live ammunition. Some fine Chilmark stone cottages can be seen in the delightful villages of **Teffont Magna** and **Teffont Evias**, a couple of miles to the east. The settlements take their name from the Anglo-Saxon words teo, meaning *"boundary"*, and funta, meaning *"brook"*; the name for the stream which connects them, the Teff, has similar roots. In both villages, the stream runs beside the main street and the houses are reached by crossing one of the series of attractive small footbridges.

An interesting open farm, **Farmer Giles Farmstead**, can be found on the western side of the minor road which connects Teffont Magna with the A303. The attractions of this 175-acre working livestock farm include a herd of 150 dairy cows, shire horses, Highland cattle, Shetland ponies, sheep, goats, rabbits and a variety of domestic fowl, all of which can be seen at close quarters.

Visitors can try their hand and milking a Jersey cow or bottle-feeding a baby lamb, or enjoy a leisurely stroll around this beautiful stretch of Wiltshire downland. There is also an interesting exhibition on the history of farming, a pond stocked with rainbow trout, a restaurant, and a children's adventure play area furnished with old tractors and modern playground equipment. (Open daily, 10.30am to 6pm between late-March and early-November; also weekends throughout the winter.)

CHAPTER THREE
Marlborough to Devizes

Devizes Castle

6
Marlborough to Devizes

Marlborough
Map 2 ref F5

8 miles S of Swindon on the A345

The historic market town of Marlborough is situated in the valley of the River Kennett on the southern edge of the Marlborough Downs. An important former coaching centre which stands at the intersection of five long-established trunk routes, it is thought to have inherited its name from *Maerl's Barrow*, an ancient burial chamber which is now contained within the grounds of the famous Marlborough College public school. William the Conqueror built a castle at Marlborough shortly after the Norman invasion and a number of early English monarchs are known to have come here to hunt in nearby Savernake Forest.

In the 17th century, the original fortification was rebuilt as a house by Inigo Jones' pupil, John Webb. It subsequently became a regular haunt of Samuel Pepys, then around 1700, it was converted into the Castle Inn and became one of the most popular stopping places on the busy coaching route between London and Bristol. Eventually, it too was incorporated into *Marlborough College* when the school was founded in 1843.

Despite having suffered three damaging fires in the late 17th century, Marlborough still possesses one of the finest main streets in the country. Reputed to be the widest in Europe, this unusually grand thoroughfare is lined with handsome Tudor houses and Georgian colonnaded shops, and also contains two imposing Perpendicular churches. A narrow passageway behind St Mary's leads to the Green, the site of an early Saxon settlement and the place where sheep fairs were held until 1893. Each year in October, a *Mop Fair* is held in commemoration of the old hiring market, an annual gathering where tradespeople looking for work would stand in the marketplace holding the tool of their trade. The best way to explore the old town is on foot and with this in mind, the tourist information office near St Peter's church has produced an excellent leaflet entitled Marlborough: A Guided Walk.

First-rate bed and breakfast accommodation is offered by Yvonne Hale at **Number Three Baywater**, a very pleasant bungalow with an attractive garden which is situated within easy walking distance of Marlborough town centre. Nicely furnished in modern style, guests are sure to enjoy their stay in this relaxed home-from-home atmosphere. Yvonne offers a warm welcome, comfortable accommodation, and one of the finest breakfasts in the district. *No. 3 Baywater, Marlborough, Wiltshire   Tel: 01672 512230*

Savernake
Map 2 ref G5
2 miles SE of Marlborough off the A346

The magnificent **Savernake Forest** lies to the southeast of Marlborough between the A4 and A346. A royal hunting forest since pre-Norman times, the 2000 acres which survive today are leased by the Marquess of Ailesbury to the Forestry Commission, making this the only ancient forest in England not to be owned by the Crown. Once under the stewardship of Sir John Seymour, it was here that Henry VIII is reputed to have met Sir John's daughter, Jane.

Savernake Forest underwent a major redevelopment in the 18th-century and its present layout owes much to the great landscaper, Capability Brown. He was responsible for cutting the broad straight swathe through the trees known as **Grand Avenue** which runs southeastwards for four miles from a distinctive crenelated toll house on the A4. He also created the striking circus at its midpoint from which eight forest walks radiate according to the points of the compass. Savernake forest is renowned for its massive oaks, beeches and Spanish chestnuts and has been designated a Site of Special Scientific Interest for its unusually diverse of flora and fauna.

Crofton
Map 2 ref G6
7 miles SE of Marlborough off the A338

To the south of Savernake forest, the A346 Marlborough to Burbage road descends into the eastern end of the Vale of Pewsey, the fertile valley which lies between the Marlborough Downs and Salisbury Plain. This broad east-west running valley also carries main London to Penzance railway line and the **Kennett and Avon Canal**. Built at the turn of the 19th century to connect Bristol with London, this ambitious inland waterway reaches its highest point near Crofton, a hamlet lying in the lanes to the east of A346.

The site is marked by a handsome Georgian engine house which contains some of the oldest and largest working *Beam Engines* in the world, including one dating from 1812. In their heyday, these magnificent steam-powered machines were capable of pumping water into the canal at a rate of eleven tons a minute. On certain days during the summer months, visitors can see spectacular working demonstrations of the engines which have been lovingly restored under the guidance of the Kennett and Avon Canal Trust.

East and West Grafton *Map 2 ref G6*

8 miles SE of Marlborough on the A338

A minor road to the south of Crofton leads over the Kennett and Avon canal to the sister communities of East and West Grafton. The latter contains one of the finest bed and breakfast establishments in this part of Wiltshire - Mayfield - the delightful home of Chris

Mayfield

and Angie Orssich. This superb thatched house is a converted 15th-century Wiltshire A-frame longhouse whose timbered brickwork dates back to Elizabethan times. The beautifully-furnished interior has a charming atmosphere, with sloping ceilings and lots of little nooks and crannies.

Full of life and character, the focal point of this comfortable family home is the spacious farmhouse kitchen where a ready supply of good wholesome food is prepared, and from where the tantalising aroma of a sizzling breakfast draws guests from the comfort of their

Wilton Windmill

beds each morning. The bedrooms are tastefully furnished and equipped with en suite facilities, and the beautiful eight-acre grounds incorporate a heated swimming pool, a Victorian fruit cage and an all-weather tennis court. A wonderful base for exploring the lovely Kingdom of Wessex with its many places of interest, Mayfield lies within easy driving distance of Bath, Cheltenham and the Cotswolds. Highly recommended. *Mayfield, West Grafton, Near Marlborough, Wiltshire Tel: 01672 811158*

Wilton
Map 2 ref G6

8 miles SE of Marlborough off the A338

A couple of miles to the east of Crofton lies the small village of Wilton. It can be reached either by car around the small lanes of the area or there is a short walk next to **Wilton Water** along a very pretty footpath. The village's main attraction, apart from being on the Wiltshire Cycleway, is the fully restored and working windmill. Regularly throughout the summer it is open to visitors and locally milled flour can be purchased on the premises.

Great Bedwyn
Map 2 ref G5

6 miles SE of Marlborough off the A4

The tomb of Sir John Seymour, the father Henry VIII's third wife, Jane Seymour, can be found in the chancel of the 11th-century church of St Mary the Virgin in Great Bedwyn, two miles to the northeast. A Victorian lamp standard on a traffic island in the centre of The Square marks the centre of this sizable village. A walk along Church Street to the south of here leads to **Lloyds' Stone Museum**, an exhibition dedicated to the skills of the English stonemason. The museum is run by the seventh generation of a family of stonemasons whose lineage can be traced back over 200 years. Items on show include a stone aeroplane with an eleven-foot wingspan, a curious assortment of tombstones, and a well-presented display on the history and secret art of stone-carving.

Little Bedwyn
Map 2 ref G5

7 miles E of Marlborough off the A4

To the northeast of Great Bedwyn, the minor road running parallel to the Kennett and Avon Canal passes beneath the site of **Chisbury Chapel**, a lonely place of worship which stands on the site of a much earlier hill fort. The attractive village of Little Bedwyn lies another mile further on, and here it is possible to cross to the southeastern side of the canal to reach **Bridge Cottage**, a delightful bed and breakfast establishment which stands right on the canal towpath. Owned by Jane and Dick Daniel, this charming establishment provides everything for a perfect holiday or weekend get-away. The property, which is over 200 years old, is constructed of mellow red brick and offers comfortable accommodation, either on the first floor of the cottage or in the Granary, an adjoining self-contained ground floor unit which can also be hired on a self-catering basis. Early morning tea is provided - a nice touch and a pleasant change from having to make one's own - along with all the usual comforts, including television and central heating. Narrowboats regularly chug

Bridge Cottage

past the bedroom window, and guests can even try boating themselves. The local pub is owned by the village residents and serves excellent food. With Marlborough only a few miles away, Bridge Cottage offers good reasonably-priced accommodation in a unique canalside setting. *Bridge Cottage, Little Bedwyn, Near Marlborough, Wiltshire Tel: 01672 870795*

Froxfield
7 miles E of Marlborough on the A4

Map 2 ref G5

Continuing northwards, the road intersects with the A4 near Froxfield, an attractive village of brick and flint buildings which contains an unusual 17th-century development known as the **Somerset Hospital**. This consists of a chapel and fifty almshouses set around a quadrangle which is entered by way of an impressive early 19th-century archway.

Wootton Rivers   *Map 2 ref F5*
4 miles S of Marlborough off the A345

To the southwest of Marlborough, the A345 Upavon road ascends past an impressive White Horse, one of several similar figures which have been cut into Wiltshire's steep chalk downland since ancient times. A couple of miles further on, a minor road to the southeast passes close to the **Martinsall Hill Fort** on its way to Wootton Rivers, an attractive village which is renowned for its highly unusual church clock. This was built by a local man from a wonderful assortment of mechanical scrap, including old bicycles, prams and farm implements, to mark the coronation of George V in 1911. Known as the **Jack Spratt Clock**, it has 24 different chimes and a clock face bearing letters instead of numbers.

Clench Farmhouse

Some of the loveliest bed and breakfast accommodation in the area can be found at **Clench Farmhouse**, a beautiful detached period house surrounded by pleasant lawned gardens and mature trees on the edge of Wootton Rivers. This is a truly delightful property, with old metal railings along the garden wall, an entrance gate, creeper-covered walls, and a tennis court and swimming pool in the grounds. Though no longer part of a working farm, the land having been sold some years ago by a previous owner, the house is tastefully furnished in genuine farmhouse style. Resident proprietor Clarissa Roe offers excellent accommodation and a delicious farmhouse breakfast. She also provides superb evening meals by prior arrangement. Despite its genuinely tranquil setting, Clench Farmhouse is conveniently situated within easy reach of Marlborough and the motorway network. *Clench Farmhouse, Wootton Rivers, Near Marlborough, Wiltshire Tel: 01672 810264*

Milton Lilbourne   Map 2 ref f6
6 miles S of Marlborough off the B3087

A minor road to the south of Wootton Rivers crosses the B3087 Pewsey to Burbage road near the village of Milton Lilbourne. A place of outstanding natural and architectural beauty, this long rambling community has a handsome village church and a collection of fine old cottages which are linked by a series of raised pavements. It also provides a good base for walks onto **Milton Hill** and to the nearby Neolithic long barrow which is known locally as the **Giant's Grave**.

Pewsey   Map 2 ref F6
7 miles S of Marlborough on the A345

The lovely old town of Pewsey lies in the heart of the vale which shares its name, two miles to the west of Milton Lilbourne. Once under the personal ownership of King Alfred the Great, a statue of the 9th-century king of Wessex stands by the crossroads in the centre of town overlooking the River Avon. The parish church was built on a foundation of early sarsen stones. Its tower was added in the 15th-century and the interior contains an unusual altar rail made from timbers belonging to the San Josef, a ship captured by Nelson in 1797. A pleasant assortment of Georgian houses and thatched cottages line Pewsey's streets which, each September, are home to a well-known West Country carnival. Half a mile north of the town centre, the A345 crosses the **Kennett and Avon Canal** at Pewsey Wharf, a former inland port whose old canal house, warehouses and docks can still be made out.

Over the years, visitors to Pewsey have enjoyed a warm welcome and a high standard of accommodation whilst staying with Brenda and Fred Trowbridge at **Well Cottage**. This picturesque thatched cottage is situated in a quiet and peaceful village setting in the Vale of Pewsey, an Area of Outstanding Natural Beauty.

It lies only 300 yards from the Kennett and Avon Canal and is surrounded by beautiful walking country. Brenda and Fred have recently improved the property and can now offer more accommodation. Brenda is a most charming lady who looks after her guests and makes them feel very much at home. Free collection from the station can be provided, if required, and evening meals are available by arrangement. Alternatively, there are several good pubs in

Well Cottage

the locality for those preferring to eat out. Ideal for longer stays, Well Cottage lies within easy reach of unspoilt countryside and is a comfortable drive from Salisbury, Swindon, Bath and Oxford. *Well Cottage, Honey Street, Pewsey, Wiltshire   Tel: 01672 851577*

Upavon
Map 2 ref F7
10 miles S of Marlborough on the A345
To the southwest of Pewsey, the A345 skirts the base of Pewsey Down before meeting the A342 Andover to Devizes road in the bustling community of Upavon. This ancient Saxon river town was the birthplace of Henry *"Orator"* Hunt, a celebrated Georgian character who became the Member of Parliament for Preston in 1830. The A345 to the south of here follows the western bank of the River Avon as it drops towards Amesbury and Stonehenge. The smaller road on the eastern bank connects a number of attractive riverside settlements, including Longstreet and Fittleton; Netheravon, on the main road, is renowned for its striking dovecote.

Marden
Map 2 ref E6
7 miles E of Devizes off the A342
The Vale of Pewsey to the northwest of Upavon is crisscrossed by a dense network of country lanes. Lying on the vale's southern mar-

gin between the A342 and the Kennett and Avon Canal, the ancient community of Marden has a 12th-century pinnacled church which is thought to have one of the oldest doors in the country. The lock is known to be at least three centuries old, the timber is thought to be as old as the church itself, and the elaborately carved door surround incorporates designs from the early Norman period. Also worth seeing is the fine chancel arch and the unusual ceiling in the nave. The village also possesses a mill which was mentioned in the Domesday Book and an imposing 18th-century manor house, **Marden Manor**.

One of the largest Neolithic henge monuments in Britain stands on a 35-acre oval site to the northeast of Marden. Dating from around 2000 BC, it has entrances on its northern and eastern sides and once contained an enormous earthwork mound, **Hatfield Barrow**, which stood 50ft high and 200ft wide at its base.

Alton Barnes and Alton Priors   *Map 2 ref E6*
6 miles SW of Marlborough off the A345

A number of attractive communities lie along the base of the chalk escarpment to the north of the Kennett and Avon Canal. Alton Barnes possesses a tiny church with a Saxon shell and a timber roof dating from the 15th century. In 1830, a mob of Luddites protesting about the introduction of agricultural machinery stormed the nearby rectory and manor house, injuring one of the rector's colleagues and requiring the militia to be called out from Marlborough and Devizes.

The largest white horse in Wiltshire can be seen on the hillside above Alton Barnes. According to local legend, the contractor who was originally commissioned to carry out the carving ran off with the £20 advance payment. Notwithstanding, work was completed in 1812 and today, the figure is visible from Old Sarum over twenty miles away to the south. A good view of the white horse can be had from the old Barge Inn which lies at the foot of Milk Hill in the village of Honey Street. The inn once incorporated a bakery and general store which served the surrounding communities for many years.

To the north of Alton Barnes, a steep lane climbs towards the summit of **Knap Hill**, the site of a New Stone Age encampment which can be reached from the road via a short footpath. Another path provides a short but fairly demanding climb to a long barrow known as **Adam's Grave** from which there are fine views in all directions. **Rybury**, the westernmost of the trio of prehistoric hill forts which lie along this stretch the chalk ridge, can be found on the far side of Milk Hill.

West Overton

Map 2 ref F5

3 miles W of Marlborough off the A4

The minor road to the north of Knap Hill crosses some dramatic downland countryside before dropping down into the valley of the upper Kennett, a locality containing one of the highest concentrations of prehistoric remains in Britain. The scattered community of West Overton stands at the foot of Overton Hill, the site of an important early Bronze Age monument known as **The Sanctuary**.

These impressive standing stones are believed to have been erected between 2000 and 1500 BC as a replacement for an earlier monument which consisted of wooden posts arranged in six concentric circles. The lost timbers, along with any standing stones missing from the later structure, have now been replaced with a series of concrete substitutes so the monument's original layout can easily be seen. The Sanctuary stands at the southeastern end of West Kennett Avenue, an ancient pathway lined with standing stones which was built to connect it to the main megalithic circles at Avebury.

Overton Hill is also the starting point of the **Ridgeway Long Distance Footpath** which runs for 85 miles through the North Wessex Downs to the Chiltern Hills. The first four-mile stretch offers a dramatic, if somewhat strenuous, ascent to the top of the 892ft **Hackpen Hill**. This is followed by a gentler walk through an undulating downland landscape littered with standing, or sarsen, stones and Bronze Age round barrows. A short diversion from the Ridgeway leads to **Fyfield Down**, the section of the Marlborough Downs whose ancient quarries provided many of the great stones which can be seen at Stonehenge. The surrounding area is now a nature reserve and walkers should keep to the marked footpaths. The spectacular **Devil's Den** long barrow lies within the reserve in a shallow hollow known as Flatford Bottom. According to legend, Satan sometimes appears here at midnight and attempts to pull down the stones using a team of white oxen.

Lockeridge

Map 2 ref F5

3 miles W of Marlborough off the A4

The village of Lockeridge lies on the southern bank of the Kennett, a mile to the east of West Overton. Situated on a minor road which runs broadly parallel to the A4 Marlborough road, this pleasant community has a good pub - the *"Who'd a Thought It"* - a school, a shop and a number of attractive old houses, but curiously no church.

East and West Kennett

Map 2 ref E5

4 miles W of Marlborough on the A4

The twin settlements of East and West Kennett are situated upstream from West Overton, a short distance to the west. A pleasant half-mile stroll from the villages crosses the River Kennett before gently ascending to the site of the **West Kennett Long Barrow**, the largest sectioned burial chamber in the country. This 4500 year-old tomb is over 330ft long, 80ft wide and 10ft high and is approached by way of a semicircular forecourt. The narrow entrance continues to be obstructed by number of colossal standing stones through which it is just possible to squeeze.

Excavations in 1956 revealed five burial chambers which together contained the remains of around forty people, including over a dozen children. The barrow is thought to have served as a tomb for around 1000 years, carbon dating having fixed a date of 2570 BC on its oldest human remains. The final sealing of the tomb, dated by pottery fragments, is believed to have taken place around 1600 BC. At East Kennett, there is another smaller and as yet unexcavated barrow which is covered in tall trees.

Silbury Hill

Map 2 ref E5

5 miles W of Marlborough on the A4

The largest prehistoric manmade mound in Europe can be found beside the A4, half a mile north of the West Kennett long barrow. The huge flat-topped cone of **Silbury Hill** stands 130ft high and covers an area of five acres. Its purpose, however, remains a mystery. Recent excavations have yielded little information about its origins, except that it was probably constructed in four stages between around 2500 BC and 100 BC. According to local legend, the structure contains a large gold statue which was hidden here by the Devil while on his way to Devizes. A more plausible theory suggests that it was created as a burial place for King Sil and his horse. Whatever its history, the uncanny presence of this curious green cone seems to dominate the surrounding landscape. Because of problems with erosion, however, members of the public are no longer permitted to climb to the top.

Avebury

Map 2 ref E4/5

6 miles W of Marlborough on the A4361

Less than a mile to the north, the ancient settlement of **Avebury** is situated at the heart of one of the most extraordinary megalithic monuments in Europe. Now designated a World Heritage Site, the village stands on a 28-acre area which is surrounded by a ring of sarsen stones almost a mile in circumference. This in turn is enclosed by a ditch and a raised bank which encircle almost 100 standing stones which are thought to date from around 2300 BC. These are believed to have been erected by the Beaker people, immigrants from continental Europe who brought with them sophisticated pottery-making skills. Ceramic fragments have been discovered throughout the locality, and some exceptional undamaged pieces have been found in the graves of their former chieftains.

Avebury Stones

A remarkable feat for its time, stones weighing as much as forty tons were dragged down from the Marlborough Downs and erected in three circles. The megaliths come in two basic shapes: tall narrow ones, which are believed to represent the male form, and broad diamond-shaped ones, which represent the female form. These characteristics have led archeologists to conclude the site was principally used for the observance of fertility rituals. Sadly, only 27 stones in the most central area remain, the others having been removed over the centuries largely to provide the village with building materials. The positions of the missing megaliths have been marked by a series of modern concrete piers.

Avebury Stone Circle was extensively excavated by Alexander Keiller during the 1930s and a museum bearing his name is located just outside the earthwork perimeter near the part-Saxon, part-Norman village church of St James. Administered by English Heritage, the ***Alexander Keiller Museum*** houses a fascinating collection of artefacts discovered at Avebury and at nearby **Windmill Hill**, a Neolithic hill fort and Bronze Age burial ground which lies in the downs a mile to the northwest. The museum is open daily, 9.30am (2pm on winter Sundays) to 6.30pm (4pm in winter), all year round.

Alexander Kieller Museum

Another interesting attraction in the village is the **Great Barn Museum**, an exhibition of Wiltshire rural life which is housed in a magnificently-restored 17th-century thatched barn. The history of such long-established rural skills as blacksmithing, thatching, cheese-making, saddlery and shepherding is documented in a unique collection of old photographs, tools and other related exhibits.

Great Barn Museum

Regular demonstrations of rural crafts take place throughout the season, and a wide choice of books, craft and food items are available in the museum shop. (Open daily, 10am to 5.30pm between mid-March and mid-November, plus weekends in winter.)

Standing almost exactly at the centre of Avebury monument, the **Guy Perkins Pottery and Showroom** is situated in a long thatched house on the opposite side of the main road from the Red Lion pub. Guy is renowned for his hand-thrown stoneware bowls and pressed geometric dishes which are fired to 1250¡C in a gas kiln. His work is robust, light in weight and beautifully made in a wide range of shapes, styles and sizes.

Perkins Ceramics

Guy is passionate about pattern, and one of his particular interests is the development of colour in high-temperature glazes. He says it is challenging to create strong vibrant finishes which retain sufficient definition on both sloping and horizontal surfaces. His work has been exhibited and sold in many of Britain's finest galleries, as well as being shown in Germany, France and Japan. Guy spent six months working and learning in Mashiko, a potters' village in Japan; time permitting, he is happy to talk about his current work and past experiences. A most interesting find, purchases made here are sure to give lasting pleasure. *Perkins Ceramics, 6 Green Street, Avebury, Near Marlborough, Wiltshire Tel: 01672 539307*

Avebury also possesses an elegant Elizabethan manor house, **Avebury Manor**, which stands on the site of a 12th-century priory.

Avebury Manor

Now under the ownership of the National Trust, it has been altered on several occasions over the centuries, particularly during the reign of Queen Anne. Major modifications were also carried out by a Colonel Jenner during in the Edwardian era. The interior contains some fine plasterwork ceilings and an interesting collection of period furniture and porcelain. The manor grounds are partly laid out as a formal garden and incorporate the remains of the medieval monastic walls, an old dovecote and some splendid topiary. (House open Tuesdays, Wednesdays, Sundays and Bank Holiday Mondays, 2pm to 5.30pm between late March and end-October.)

Those looking for first-rate bed and breakfast accommodation in

Westbrook

historic Avebury should make a point of finding **Westbrook**, the delightful home of Mrs Sheila Moss. Set in a quiet location in the heart of wonderful countryside, this charming cottage is full of genuine character - a real piece of old England. The guest accommodation is tastefully furnished and equipped with en suite bathroom, colour television and tea/coffee making facilities, and the breakfasts are out of this world! A little gem for which advance booking is recommended. *Westbrook, Bray Street, Avebury, Near Marlborough, Wiltshire Tel: 01672 539377*

Winterbourne Monkton

Map 2 ref E4

7 miles W of Marlborough on the A4361

The A361 to the north of Avebury leads into the western margin of the Marlborough Downs. Winterbourne Monkton, a mile and a half to the north, is an attractive village with a tiny church which has an unusual shingled belfry supported on timbers sited within the building.

The A361 to the southwest of Avebury ascends onto the dramatic upland spur known as North Down. Approximately halfway to Devizes, the road crosses the ridge which carries the ancient **Wansdyke Path**. This once-spectacular earthwork is thought to have been constructed in the late 6th century by the Britons as a defence against the Saxons, and then strengthened two centuries later by the west Saxons as a defence against the Vikings. Consisting of a single raised bank and ditch, it once stretched for over fifty miles from the Berkshire border to the coast of northern Somerset. The twelve-mile eastern section from Savernake Forest to Morgan's Hill, near Calne provides some of the most spectacular archeological walking in England. An excellent view of the Wansdyke itself can be enjoyed from the top of **Tan Hill**, a viewpoint above the village of All Cannings in the heart of the Vale of Pewsey.

Bishops Cannings   Map 1 ref D5
2 miles NE of Devizes on the A361

A mile and a half beyond the Wansdyke, it is worth making a short detour off the A361 to visit the old ecclesiastical community of Bishops Cannings. The village is so-called because the Bishops of Salisbury once owned a manor here, and as a likely consequence, the somewhat oversized parish church bears a striking resemblance to Salisbury cathedral, complete with fine stone carving and tall tapering spire. The organ was donated to the church in 1809 by Captain Cook's navigator, William Bayley, who was born locally. The building also contains an unusual meditation seat which is inscribed with some cautionary words in Latin on the subject of sin and death.

According to local legend, the term *"Wiltshire Moonraker"* has its origin in Bishops Cannings. In the 16th century, a government excise patrol discovered two local men combing a village pond with a rake on the night of a full moon. When asked what they were doing, they villagers pointed to the moon's reflection replied that they were trying to scrape the thick yellow cheese from the surface. Convinced they had lost their senses, the excisemen roared with laughter and rode off into the night, leaving the local men to get on with their task of retrieving their cache of contraband liquor from the bottom of the pond.

A hollow in the downs to the west of Bishops Cannings was the scene of a bloody Civil War battle on 13 July 1643. The Royalist forces under Prince Rupert's brother, Maurice, defeated the Parliamentarian forces at Roundway Down. Local legend has it that each year on the anniversary of the battle, the cries of the dead can be heard emanating from a burial ditch beside the battlefield. One mile further south, a stroll to the beech trees on top of **Roundway Hill** provides some spectacular views over the surrounding downland landscape.

Horton   Map 2 ref E5
3 miles NE of Devizes off the A361
The small village of Horton lies on the eastern side of the A361, a mile to the southeast of Bishops Cannings. This is the location of **Part Acre**, a comfortable bed and breakfast establishment which is situated in a quiet location just three miles from the centre of Devizes. Proprietor Shirley Jones is a lovely lady who provides good reasonably-priced accommodation and a genuine old-fashioned welcome.
Part Acre, Horton, Near Devizes, Wiltshire   Tel: 01380 860261

Devizes   Map 1 ref D6
13 miles SW of Marlborough on the A361
The sizable former market town of Devizes stands at the junction of the A361 and A342, at the western end of the Vale of Pewsey. By the standards of many other settlements in the locality, this is a relatively modern town, having been founded by the William the Conqueror's nephew, Bishop Osmund, in 1080. The bishop was responsible for building a timber castle between the lands of two powerful manors. This odd situation gave the town its name, which is derived from the Latin *ad divisas* meaning *"at the boundaries"*. After the original wooden structure burnt down, Roger, Bishop of Sarum, built a stone castle in 1138 which remained in place until it was compulsorily dismantled at the end of the English Civil War. The **Devizes Castle** that can be seen today is a 19th-century reproduction which is not open to visitors.

Bishop Roger also built two fine churches in Devizes: St Mary's in New Park Street and St John's near the site of the old castle. The latter was built around 1130 and features a fine Norman tower and a number of contemporary arches with characteristic zigzag carving. The churchyard contains some interesting tombs and is surrounded by a number of lovely old buildings, including a 17th-century sexton's house. Elsewhere in the town, Long Street is lined with elegant Georgian dwellings and also contains the Wiltshire Archeological and Natural History Society's award-winning **Devizes Museum**. This houses a superb collection of historic artefacts from the locality, including those from the important archeological sites

St John's Church, Devizes

of Avebury and Stonehenge.

The popularity of Italian restaurants has grown immensely in recent years, and **Franco's Ristorante and Pizzeria** in in the centre of Devizes is one that is certainly worth a visit. Franco and Anna are delightful hosts who serve the finest Italian cuisine at very reasonable prices. The restaurant has a marvellous atmosphere and offers a wide selection of traditional antipasti, pasta and

Franco's Ristorante

pizzas, along with an extensive range of meat, poultry and fish dishes, both on the regular menu and as specials of the day. Of course, no meal would be complete without a tantalising dessert such as zabaglione, tiramisu, or one of the many variations of ice cream, while for those without a sweet tooth, there is always cheese and crusty bread! *Franco's Ristorante, 6 Old Swan Yard, High Street, Devizes, Wilts Tel: 01380 724007*

Many of the finest buildings in Devizes are situated in and around the old Market Place. These include the town hall, the corn exchange and the handsome 16th-century coaching inn, the Bear Hotel. The **Market Place** is also the site of an unusual market cross, one panel of which is inscribed with the sobering story of Ruth Pierce, a market stall-holder who, in 1753, was accused of swindling her customers. When an angry throng assembled, Ruth stood up in front of them and pleaded, *"May I be struck dead if I am lying"*, at

Market Cross, Devizes

which point she fell to the ground and expired.

The Kennett and Avon Canal passes along the northern edge of Devizes. This impressive inland waterway was built to link London with Bristol, and at that time, **Devizes Wharf** was a flourishing commercial centre through which the majority of the town's goods passed. Today, the wharf is a more peaceful place, though in recent years it has undergone something of a rejuvenation. Several of the old warehouses have been renovated and are now occupied by organisations such as the tourist information office, the **Wharf Theatre** and the **Canal Interpretation Centre**, which provides a fascinating insight into the background and history of the canal. Each year in March, the famous **Devizes to Westminster International Canoe Race** starts near here and follows the Kennett and Avon Canal and River Thames all the way to London.

The **Kennett and Avon Canal Trust** was formed more than thirty years ago to restore the disused Kennett and Avon Canal from Reading to Bristol, both as a through navigation and as a public

Kennet and Avon Canal Trust

amenity. The many years of campaigning, fund-raising and volunteer work were rewarded when this impressive inland waterway was re-opened by Her Majesty the Queen in 1990.

However, the work is not yet complete, and major improvements to the structure of the canal and its water supply are essential if the waterway is to enjoy a sustainable future. An important water recycling scheme is nearing completion and the Trust, in partnership with British Waterways and the riparian local authorities, is continuing its work to safeguard and improve navigation. *Kennett and Avon Canal Trust, Canal Centre, Couch Lane, Devizes, Wiltshire Tel: 01380 721279*

Kennet & Avon Canal

Pleasure boats offering trips on the canal operate from Hungerford, Crofton, Pewsey, Bradford-on-Avon and Bath. Crewed by fully-trained volunteer staff, they conform to government safety regulations. Further information on public and charter trips, along with facilities for wedding receptions and private parties, can be obtained by contacting the Trust. Devizes' ***Kennett and Avon Canal Museum*** is well worth visiting, as is the unique water-wheel driven pumping station at Claverton and the coal-fired, steam-driven pumping station at Crofton. The latter houses the oldest working beam engine in the world, still in its original building and still doing its original job. The Trust also warmly welcomes new subscription members.

Strongly recommended is a walk along the canal towpath to the famous ***Caen Hill Locks***. The land to the west of Devizes falls 200 feet within the space of two miles, a descent which posed a significant problem to the canal's engineer John Rennie. He solved the difficulty by constructing a giant staircase of sixteen locks, so tightly-spaced that they scarcely seem a narrowboat-length apart. In total, a series of 29 double-gated locks were needed to traverse the whole valley, a sequence through which the hardest working bargees took half-a-day to pass. In recent years, the locks have undergone an extensive programme of restoration which aims to reopen this stretch of the canal to water-borne traffic by the year 2000. An excellent view of the flight of locks can be had from a white-painted bridge over the canal which lies a few hundred yards along the gravel towpath from Devizes wharf.

Delightful bed and breakfast accommodation lying within fifteen minutes' walk of the Market Place can be found in Wick Lane on the southern side of Devizes. The impressive home of Roger and Laura Stratton, ***The Gatehouse*** offers guests the choice of bed and breakfast accommodation in the main house, or self-catering accommodation in a well-appointed ground floor annex. B & B guests can choose from a double room with en suite facilities, or a twin or single room with a shared private bathroom. All are spacious, pleasantly decorated, and equipped with TV, radio-alarm, hair dryer and hospitality tray.

B & B guests are warmly invited to relax in the beautiful house and large garden, and in the morning, a full English or continental breakfast is prepared to their individual requirements and served in the dining room overlooking the gardens. The holiday annex has been awarded 4 keys highly-commended by the English Tourist Board and is comprehensively equipped for two. Set well back from

The Gatehouse

the road in a quiet lane with plenty of off-road parking, the Gatehouse enjoys a delightfully tranquil location and is an ideal base for exploring Bath, Salisbury and the idyllic unspoilt villages and countryside of rural Wiltshire. *The Gatehouse, Wick Lane, Devizes, Wiltshire Tel/Fax: 01380 725283*

Another recommended bed and breakfast establishment offering good value accommodation, can be found in nearby Downlands Road. Resident proprietor Mrs Rosemary Milne-Day has been in business for fifteen years and welcomes families and well-behaved pets. Her house, **Asta**, lies within easy reach of the many surrounding places of interest, but is unsuitable for smokers. *Asta Bed and Breakfast, 66 Downlands Road, Devizes, Wiltshire Tel: 01380 722546*

Potterne   *Map 1 ref D6*
1 mile S of Devizes on the A360

A couple of miles to the south of Devizes, the A360 passes through the lovely old village of Potterne, the location of an interesting exhibition of antique fire engines and fire-fighting equipment. The village also contains some fine old buildings, including a 13th-century church with a Saxon font and the 500 year-old **Porch House**, a handsome black-and-white timber-framed structure which in its lifetime has served as a priest's home, an alehouse, a bakery and an army billet.

Potterne is also home to an impressive thatched inn, the **George and Dragon**. A handsome building with a history stretching back over four centuries, it is reckoned that Cromwell still owes £6.50 for billeting his troops here! The interior is full of character, with a friendly atmosphere and a collection of interesting pictures and historic photographs around the bar. The inn run by David and Jenny Wood, charming hosts who offer a full range of Wadworth's ales and

George and Dragon

beers from the wood, along with good home-cooked food and first-rate bed and breakfast accommodation. There is also a beer garden and a skittle alley, and children and pets are most welcome. *George and Dragon, Potterne, Near Devizes, Wiltshire Tel: 01380 722139*

Worton
Map 1 ref D6

3 miles SW of Devizes off the A360

A country lane to the southwest of Potterne leads to the attractive community of Worton. Situated within a lovely treed churchyard, the church here is unusual in this part of Wiltshire for not having a tower or spire.

The village also possesses a delightful country pub, the **Rose and Crown**, which was first recorded as a cider house in a census of public houses in 1726 though it was known to have existed as a blacksmith's and ale house before then, The original buildings remain, as do the old fireplaces and low ships beams - they really are low so do watch out! Since coming here in May 1996, Tracey and Brian Greene have really turned around the fortunes of the only pub in the village. Now at the heart of the local community, the Rose and Crown is well known for having the best skittles alley in the area and some 20 men's, ladies and mixed teams are based here. Competition is fierce in this part of Wiltshire with, at the height of the season, some 7,000 men around Devizes out playing this traditional pub game. When there is not a match on, anyone can try their skill in the alley but for those who like something a little less energetic, there are plenty of other traditional pub games to play, such as cribbage and dominoes.

Rose and Crown

Before *"retiring"* Brian was a master chef in the Army and, with Tracey's help, he provides an excellent range of freshly prepared, cooked to order meals, served in either the cosy dining room or the bar. Ranging from delicious sandwiches to full a la carte and with a daily specials board, there is always plenty to tempt even the most jaded palate. However, it is the interesting and unusual list of curries that has really put the pub on the culinary map. The curry menu does not only feature the more well known dishes such as mild Korma and hot Vindaloo, but also curries from Morocco, Thailand and elsewhere. All are served with their traditional accompaniments and make a tasty change from the norm. The Rose and Crown is also developing a small, but select, list of European wines and there is always a good selection of real ale on tap. Along with a beer garden, children's play area and plenty of parking, this is certainly a pub not to be missed. *Rose and Crown, 108 High Street, Worton, Near Devizes, Wiltshire   Tel: 01380 724202*

Erlestoke
Map 1 ref D7

5 miles SW of Devizes on the B3098

A lane to the southwest of Worton passes through the attractive community of Marston before arriving in Erlestoke, a sheltered settlement lying on the B3098 Westbury to Market Lavington road. The layout of the village was much altered in the late 18th century when the land surrounding its new manor house was emparked by the London-based landscape architect, William Eames. About a century later, the old village church was replaced by the Gothic Perpendicular-style building which can be seen today. Today, Erlestoke provides a good base for exploring Salisbury Plain, whose sombre form rises dramatically to the south.

West Lavington
Map 1 ref D7

5 miles S of Devizes on the A360

Three miles to the east, the lovely old community of West Lavington has a famous school which was founded in the mid 16th century by the local lords of the manor, the Dauntseys. The attractive wisteria-covered manor house stands adjacent to the late 12th-century village church. The Dauntsey family also constructed the handsome almshouses to the northeast of the church which were subsequently rebuilt in brick in the 1830s.

Salisbury Plain
Map 1 ref D7/8

8 miles S of Devizes on the A360

The A360 to the south of West Lavington crosses the central area of Salisbury Plain, an extensive area of chalk downland which is largely owned by the Ministry of Defence. Indeed, some 92,000 acres make up the **Salisbury Plain Military Training Area,** one third of which is regularly used by the army, either for live firing or as impact areas. As a consequence, most of the downs are permanently closed to the public, although the MoD do allow access to some of the prohibited sectors on a limited number of days each year.

There are believed to be 17,000 archeological sites within the military area, many of which are under the protection of special management agreements. The training ground also incorporates

nine Sites of Special Scientific Interest which are home to a wide
variety of wild flora and fauna. Paradoxically, many of these rare
chalkland habitats are particularly stable, having remained undisturbed for decades despite the ever-present threat from bombs and
shells. The army has also been responsible for planting over three
and a half million trees here since they first took over in 1897.

Urchfont   *Map 1 ref E6*
3 miles SE of Devizes on the B3098

The B3098 to the northeast of West Lavington connects a series of
attractive villages which lie along the northern margin of Salisbury
Plain. Perhaps most notable is Urchfont, a peaceful community
which possesses a picturesque duck pond, an exceptionally fine if
much-altered 13th-century parish church, and an elegant William
and Mary manor house which once belonged to William Pitt and
has since been converted to an educational institution.

CHAPTER FOUR
Chippenham to Trowbridge

Steeple Ashton

6
Chippenham to Trowbridge

Chippenham

Map 1 ref C4

18 miles W of Marlborough on the A4

The historic settlement and charming old market town of Chippenham was founded on the banks of the Bristol Avon around 600 AD by the Saxon King Cyppa from whom the town gets its name. Within 250 years it had become an important administrative and hunting centre in King Alfred's Wessex. At the heart of present-day Chippenham is the ancient market place which still hosts a flourishing weekly market every Friday.

The streets of Chippenham contain a number of fine old buildings, including the 15th-century twin-gabled town hall with its unusual wooden turret. The half-timbered **Yelde Hall** was used by the Bailiff and Burgesses of the *Chippenham Hundred* until 1841; having been extensively restored, the building was reopened as a museum of local history in 1963. The museum contains a number of interestingly arranged rooms, including one which has been refurbished as the old town lock up. Open Mondays to Saturdays, 10am to 12.30pm and 2pm to 4.30pm between mid-March and end-October. Admission free

Of the four churches in Chippenham, St Andrew's is the oldest. It was founded during Saxon times, and although little from this period now remains, it contains some fine monuments from the 13th- and 15th centuries. There is also an exquisite stained-glass window and several references to the Hungerford family, the local lords of the manor. St Paul's Church in Malmesbury Road was built in Gothic revival style by architect Giles Gilbert Scott in 1855.

Other noteworthy buildings in Chippenham include the handsome early-19th-century structure, **Ivy House** and **The Grove**, the

Sheldon Manor

home of a short-lived spa during the 18th-century. At Hardenhuish Hill (pronounced *Harnish)* on the edge of Chippenham, John Wood the Younger of Bath built the Georgian church of St Nicholas on the site of a ruined mediaeval church. Completed in 1779, it is noted for its elegant Venetian windows.

The low-lying flood plain to the east of Chippenham contains an extraordinary feat of medieval civil engineering, the four and a half mile long raised footpath known as ***Maud Heath's Causeway***. This remarkable walkway consisting of 64 brick and stone arches was built at the end of the 15th century at the bequest of Maud Heath, a market trader who died a relatively wealthy woman after having lived most of her life as a poor pedlar. Maud never forgot the many times she had to trudge, often wet through, with her basket of wares from her home in the lovely old village of Bremhill to Chippenham. The land and houses she left in her will were sufficient to provide funds not only for the building and upkeep of the causeway, which is perhaps best seen near the hamlet of Kellaways, but also for the present-day river bridge. A wonderful statue of Maud, her basket at her side, stands overlooking the flood plain at Wick Hill.

A mile or so to the south of Chippenham lies the historic country house of ***Sheldon Manor***. A manor has existed here since the late 12th-century when the lands of the old Chippenham Manor were divided into three (the lordship of the Chippenham Hundred was awarded to Sheldon). With parts of the present-day house, including the porch, dating from the late 13th century, the building has been continuously occupied since 1424, the year the Hungerford family first acquired the estate. After remaining in their family for over 250 years, the house changed hands several times before being bought by the current owning family in 1917. Sheldon Manor is open to the public on Thursdays, Sundays and Bank Holiday Mondays; garden 12.30pm to 6pm, house 2pm to 6pm. Admission charge payable.

Calne
Map 1 ref D4/5

6 miles E of Chippenham on the A4

Lying in the sheltered valley of the River Marden, the former weaving centre of Calne stands at the busy junction of the A4 and A3102, six miles to the north of Devizes and 4 miles to the east of Chippenham. The town has an imposing 12th to 15th-century parish church, some fine old almshouses situated in Kingsbury Street, and an impressive coaching inn, the Lansdown Arms, which was built in the 18th century on the site of an earlier inn, the old

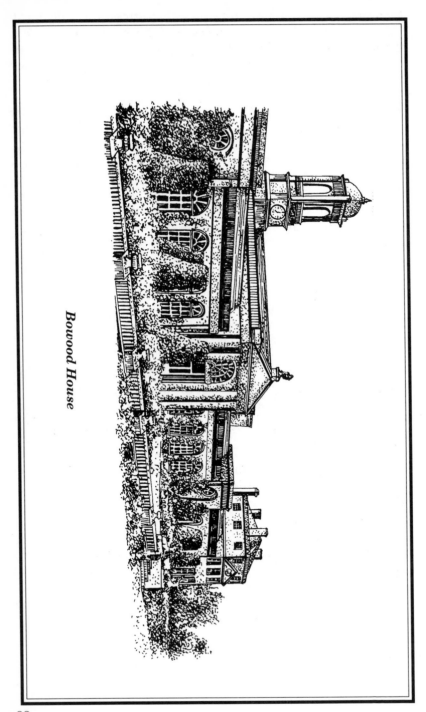

Bowood House

brewhouse of which can still be seen in the yard. In more recent times, Calne became known as a meat-curing centre which produced a celebrated range of Wiltshire cooked meats and bacon.

Cherhill   *Map 1 ref D5*
9 miles E of Chippenham on the A4

The long straggling village of Cherhill lies on the edge of the downs, three miles to the east of Calne. Now bypassed by the A4, this peaceful community has a hidden 14th to 15th-century church and an excellent pub, the Black Horse, which is the only inn to survive from the days when Cherhill was an important staging post on the busy London to Bristol coaching route. The character of the village was very different in the 18th century when an infamous band of robbers known as the **Cherhill Gang** regularly used to accost passing travellers. An encounter with the gang was said to be particularly startling, owing to their habit of removing all their clothes to avoid being recognised.

The chalk ridge to the south of the village known as **Cherhill Down** is the site of a famous white horse which was cut into the hillside by Dr Christopher Alsop in 1790. The nearby Lansdown Monument dates from 1845 and was built on the instructions of the Third Marquess of Lansdown to commemorate his ancestor, Sir William Petty. This exposed hilltop is also the site of the ancient Iron Age hill fort, **Oldbury Castle**. Now under the ownership of the National Trust, this extensive earthwork enjoys magnificent views over the Marlborough Downs. The Trust has also recently acquired nearby **Calstone Coombes**, a spectacular folded landscape which offers some magnificent opportunities for walking.

Bowood   *Map 1 ref D5*
4 miles E of Chippenham off the A4

The tranquil community of Derry Hill lies between the A4 and A342, two miles to the west of Calne and just east of Chippenham. The village is the entrance point to **Bowood House**, an elegantly-proportioned country mansion standing within extensive grounds which contain the last remnants of Chippenham Forest. The house was completely rebuilt in 1754 and has undergone a series of alterations since. Designed in part by Robert Adam, the interior includes an impressive library and the laboratory where Joseph Priestley first identified oxygen in 1774.

Bowood House is also renowned for its extensive art collection. Along with many fine watercolours, sculptures and costumes, it contains a unique collection of relics from the Indian subcontinent which was accumulated by the present owner's great-grandfather when he served as the Viceroy of India between 1888-94. The orangery has also been remodelled and is now a delightful picture gallery.

The magnificent grounds of Bowood were laid out in the 18th century by the legendary landscaper, Capability Brown. They cover more than 1000 acres and incorporate a series of delightful woodland walks which are particularly spectacular during the rhododendron season. They also contain over 150 species of well-labelled trees and a beautiful ornamental lake with an Italianate cascade, along with a restaurant, shop and children's adventure play area. The house and grounds are open daily, 11am to 6pm between late March and end-October.

Sandy Lane   Map 1 ref D5
4 miles SE of Chippenham on the A342
The charming community of Sandy Lane is situated a mile to the south of Bowood House, just off the A342 Chippenham to Devizes road. The village contains one of the few thatched churches in England, is also worth visiting for its fine collection of traditional cottages and handsome George Inn.

Lacock   Map 1 ref C5
4 miles S of Chippenham on the A 350
A minor road to the west of Sandy Lane leads to the exquisite National Trust-owned village of Lacock. Preserved as only an estate village can be, the buildings here are all reputed to be 18th century or older. A stroll around the quadrangle of streets reveals a delightful assortment of mellow stone buildings, including the famous Red Lion Hotel in the High Street. Another inn worth mentioning is the George, one of the oldest continuously licensed premises in the country. The village is regularly used a period film location, and with this in mind the Trust have taken steps to ensure that all cables run underground and all references to the modern era are kept well out of sight.

One of the area's loveliest and most atmospheric places to stay or enjoy a meal, can be found in Lacock's main Church Street. The unusually-named **Sign of the Angel** is a superb 14th-century half-timbered inn which has been run as a top-class guesthouse and restaurant by the Levis family for over four decades. With its low doorways, timber beams, oak panelling, antique furniture and open log fires, the interior is filled with genuine character and charm. The establishment is now jointly owned and run by Lorna Levis and George Hardy, friendly and experienced hosts who provide a warm welcome, charming hospitality, and the very finest food and drink.

The Sign of the Angel is renowned for its outstanding cuisine, all of which is freshly-prepared using fresh local produce wherever possible. Diners can eat inside, or have lunch or a quiet drink by the stream at the foot of the beautiful flower-filled garden to the rear.

Sign of the Angel

The accommodation too is of a very high standard. The guest bedrooms are delightfully decorated and full of atmosphere, yet are equipped with the full range of up-to-date facilities, including en suite bathrooms. Six of the ten bedrooms are located in the main inn, and four in a lovely old cottage set within the garden. *The Sign of the Angel, 6 Church Street, Lacock, Nr Chippenham, Wiltshire Tel: 01249 730230 Fax: 01249 730527*

Another of Lacock's recommended enterprises, the **Lacock Bakery**, is situated just a few doors along from the Sign of the Angel. Run by Jean Sheard and her daughter Debbie, this celebrated bakery and coffee shop occupies a lovely old building dating from the 14th-century which is leased from the National Trust. Fresh bread is baked on the premises each day, along with a wonderful assortment of homemade cakes, scones and pastries. Specialities of the house include a delicious Lardy Cake, which is made to a secret recipe, and a range of English preserves which are prepared using the finest traditional ingredients. Visitors can enjoy a delicious

Lacock Bakery

morning coffee in the lovely atmosphere of this friendly family-run establishment where the pleasant and helpful staff are clothed in Victorian dress. Continuing the family connection is eldest daughter Jacqui, who in partnership with David, owns Sheard and Hudson, a firm producing all the design and artwork for the bakery's signs and labels. *Lacock Bakery, 8 Church Street, Lacock, Wiltshire Tel: 01249 730457*

Situated a little further along Church Street, **King John's Hunting Lodge** has parts dating from the turn of the 13th-century, which almost certainly makes it the oldest house in Lacock. Much of its original cruck beam structure can be seen on the first floor, whilst the rear of building was added in Tudor times. King John was Lord of the Manor of nearby Melksham and frequently indulged his passion for hunting in the adjoining forest. There being no manor house at Melksham it is likely that the King made regular use of his hunting lodge at Lacock.

Eight centuries later, the tradition of hospitality is maintained by present-day proprietor Margaret Vaughan, who offers comfortable accommodation in the relaxed and friendly atmosphere of this delightful refurbished property. A real sanctuary from the stresses and strains of modern life, guest rooms are equipped with en suite bathrooms and tea/coffee facilities, and a full English breakfast with homemade breads is served at a time to suit guests. Evening meals, if required, can be enjoyed in one of the many local pubs and restaurants in the village. King John's Hunting Lodge is also renowned for its delicious traditional English cream teas which are served in

King John's Hunting Lodge

the delightful secluded garden in summer, or in the Garden Tearoom, with its roaring log fire, in winter. The menu features local clotted and Jersey creams, homemade jams and preserves, along with scones, cakes, cheese muffins and teacakes which are baked daily on the premises. *King John's Hunting Lodge, 21 Church Street, Lacock, Near Chippenham, Wiltshire Tel: 01249 730313*

Lacock also possesses an exceptional 15th-century church, **St Cyriacs**, which contains some superb internal features, including a fan-vaulted chapel, some fine stained glass, the tomb of Sir William Sharington, and a memorial brass of Robert Baynard and his wife surrounded by their fifteen kneeling children.

The entire village once belonged to the estate of ***Lacock Abbey***, an Augustinian nunnery which was founded in 1232 by Ela, Countess of Salisbury. Following the death of her father, Ela was married to Richard the Lionheart's stepbrother, William Longsword, to whom she bore several children. He too died soon after returning

Fox Talbot's Window

from battle, and in her grief, she founded the abbey where she lived for the next 35 years. Like all monastic houses, Lacock was dissolved by Henry VIII in 1539; however, the original cloisters, chapter house, sacristy and kitchens have survived to this day.

Much of the remainder of the present-day building dates from the mid 16th century when the abbey was acquired by Sir William Sharington. The new owner constructed an impressive country house around the abbey's medieval core, which he left largely intact with the exception of the chapel which he demolished to make room for a stable block. He was also responsible for building the elegant octagonal tower which overlooks the nearby River Avon.

In 1574, Lacock Abbey passed to the Talbot family against the wishes of the Sharingtons. Indeed, they were so dismayed when they discovered the heir to the estate, Olive Sharington, intended to marry John Talbot they withheld their permission. On hearing their marriage had been disallowed, poor Olive was so distraught that she leapt from the roof towards the outstretched arms of her lover. Fortunately, the combined action of her billowing undergarments and young John's heroic fielding saved her, and she was eventually given permission to wed the man of her choice. The house then remained in the Talbot family until being ceded to the National Trust in 1944. The beautiful wooded grounds contain an 18th-century summerhouse and a Victorian rose garden, and there are also several interesting outbuildings, including an old bakehouse, a clockhouse brewery and a 16th-century stable courtyard with half-timbered gables. (Open daily except Tuesdays, 1pm to 5.30pm between late March and early November.)

Perhaps the most eminent member of the Talbot family was the pioneering photographer, *William Henry Fox Talbot*, who carried out most of his experiments at Lacock in the 1830s. Indeed, one of the world's earliest photographs shows a detail of a latticed oriel window belonging to the abbey. Widely considered to be the inventor of the modern photographic negative, his many innovative discoveries are celebrated at the *Fox Talbot Museum*, an absorbing museum which is housed in a magnificent 16th-century tithe barn near the abbey gates. (Open daily, 11am to 5.30pm between 1 March and 1 November.)

Really delightful bed and breakfast accommodation is offered by Rachel Joad at *Videl*, an attractive modern establishment set within lovely countryside on the eastern edge of Lacock. The prize-winning gardens are a picture, and Rachel maintains a small nursery where a variety of plants can be purchased. English Tourist Board

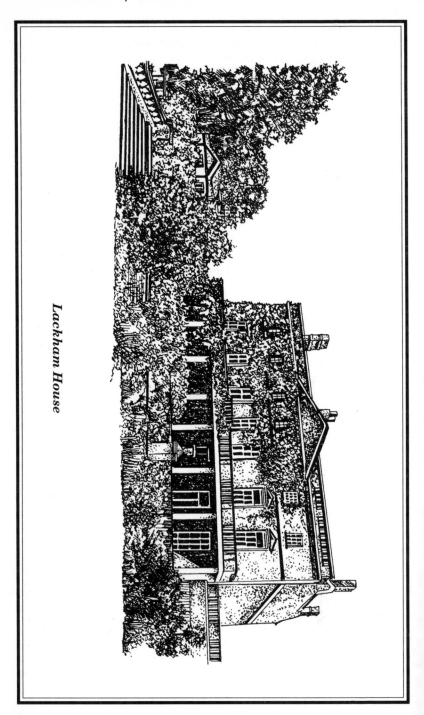

Lackham House

commended, the accommodation consists of a family room with en-suite facilities, and a twin room with private bathroom; both are

Videl Bed and Breakfast

comfortable and appointed to a high standard. Children are wel-come and pets can usually be accommodated. After waking up to the peaceful sounds of the countryside, guests are set up for the day with a delicious Wiltshire breakfast. *Videl Bed and Breakfast, 6a Bewley Lane, Lacock, Wiltshire   Tel: 01249 730279*

The beautiful ***Lackham Gardens*** are situated a mile to the north of Lacock on the A350 Chippenham road. Occupying an estate which was established prior to the Domesday Book, the gardens were land-

Vintage Farm Buildings at Lackham
Gardens and Museum

scaped in the 18th century in a style influenced by Capability Brown. The grounds incorporate a well-labelled rose collection, a long herbaceous border, glass houses, and a series of walled gardens which are renowned for their summer vegetables and striking floral displays. There is also a coffee shop, plant sales area, adventure playground, farming museum, rare breeds collection, and a pleasant woodland walk to the river. (Open daily, 11am to 5pm between Easter and end October.)

Corsham
Map 1 ref B4

3 miles Sw of Chippenham off the A4

The ancient town of Corsham lies between the A350 and A4, three miles to the west of Lacock. Founded before the days of the Romans, over the centuries the settlement grew into an important weaving and cloth-making centre. The old High Street is lined with mellow cream-coloured Bath-stone buildings, many of which date from the 17th and 18th centuries. Among the most impressive are the pedimented **Hungerford Almshouses** which were built in 1668 by the local lady of the manor, Dame Margaret Hungerford. The former warden's house, with its elegant bell tower and magnificent carved porch, is particularly attractive. The old schoolhouse standing adjacent to the almshouses is a charming period piece which retains its original classroom layout, seating and pulpit-like schoolmaster's desk.

The row of gabled Flemish-style weavers' cottages which can be seen at the other end of the High Street is characteristic of Corsham's prosperous heyday. The nearby St Bartholomew's church was built in the 12th century on the site of an earlier Saxon chapel. Despite being added to on a number of occasions and being extensively restored in 1874, the building retains a surprising number of interesting period features, both inside and out.

A good place to have a bite to eat before visiting Corsham's most famous attraction, Corsham Court, can be found at No. 55 the High Street. Occupying a handsome building in the centre of town which dates back to 1906, **Audrey's** is situated just 100 yards from its imposing entrance. This spacious tearoom is open every day for morning coffee, lunch and afternoon tea, and offers a range of home-cooked food which is both delicious and excellent value. The menu is changed regularly and features such imaginative dishes as bacon hotpot. A good homemade soup is also always available, along with a range of appetising cakes and pastries to tempt the palate. *Audrey's, 55 High Street, Corsham, Wiltshire   Tel: 01249 714931*

Saxon monarchs visited the old royal manor at Corsham long before the Norman invasion. The present *Corsham Court* is a magnificent Elizabethan mansion with a striking pedimented gateway which was built in 1582 by *"Customer"* Smythe, a high-ranking Collector of Customs in Queen Elizabeth I's London treasury; later ad-

Corsham Court

ditions were made during the Georgian era by John Nash. The surrounding grounds were laid out by the famous 18th-century landscaper, Capability Brown, with subsequent contributions by Humphrey Repton. The gardens contain an unusual Gothic-style bathhouse and a large number of semi-tame peacocks which occasionally strut out of the grounds and down the High Street.

The present owners, the Methuen family, originally acquired Corsham Court to accommodate and display their outstanding collection of 16th and 17th-century paintings and furniture. A superb setting in which to view some of the finest works of art in the country, the house and grounds are open to visitors every day, except Mondays and Fridays, from 2pm to 6pm (earlier in winter) between mid-January and mid-December.

Delightful bed and breakfast accommodation in quintessentially English surroundings can be found at the *Old Parsonage* on the northwestern edge of Corsham. Situated on the main A4 Bath road in the historic hamlet of Pickwick, this handsome detached residence has a charming garden to the rear planted in old-fashioned country cottage style. Resident proprietor Joan Webb has been providing a warm welcome for her guests for over two decades. Her house is comfortable and well-appointed, with an attractively-furnished guest lounge and separate dining room.

Each of the three guest bedrooms is spacious and full of character, and one is equipped with its own shower and hand-basin en suite. Mrs Webb provides her guests with a superb full English breakfast with all the traditional trimmings which is substantial enough to

The Old Parsonage

keep hunger at bay for most of the day. The Old Parsonage is located within easy reach of Corsham Court, Lacock Abbey and Sheldon Manor, and provides the ideal base for visiting the many renowned attractions of Chippenham and Bath. *The Old Parsonage, 4 Pickwick, Corsham, Wilts Tel: 01249 713462*

Situated in Park Lane on the southwestern edge of Corsham, **The Underground Quarry** offers visitors a truly unique experience. Well worth a visit, this unusual attraction is the only shaft stone mine in the world which is open to the public. Here, generations of quarrymen dug the fashionable honey coloured Bath stone which was used to create the fine buildings of Bath, London and countries around the world. Helmets, lamps and an experienced guide are provided to make the underground tour a safe and fascinating experience. *Underground Quarry, Park Lane, Corsham, Wiltshire Tel: 01249 716288*

Box
Map 1 ref B5
6 miles SW of Chippenham on the A4

Three miles to the southwest of Corsham, the scattered community of Box lies on the A4 midway between Chippenham and Bath. Like Corsham, the settlement has been inhabited since Roman times and the remains of buildings from this period lie dotted throughout the locality. The village has long been renowned as a source of high quality Bath stone which continues to be quarried nearby.

Box is perhaps best known, however, for having given its name to one of the most remarkable feats of civil engineering of the early Victorian era, *Box Tunnel*. The 1.8 mile-long railway tunnel took five years to build and when completed in 1841, it was the longest example of its kind in the world. The west portal can be seen from a viewing point on the A4 where, in 1987, a plaque was erected on the completion of a major cleaning and restoration programme. According to local legend, the sun shines through the entire length of the tunnel on only one occasion each year - sunrise on April 9, the birthday of its creator, Isambard Kingdom Brunel.

Monkton Farleigh
Map 1 ref B5
9 miles SW of Chippenham off the A4

Situated in the lanes two miles to the southwest of Box, the village of Monkton Farleigh possesses a fine Norman church. The structure dates from around 1200 and incorporates some exceptional period carving, most notably around the inner door and archway in the north porch. Much of the detail carries the familiar zigzag pattern characteristic of the Norman era. The church contains some striking internal features, including an attractive Elizabethan carved pulpit and some fine pre-Reformation carving in the choir stalls. The sturdy tower dates from the second half of the 13th century and is built to a traditional saddleback design.

Another saddleback tower can be found on the church at Atworth, a long scattered village spread along the A365 Box to Melksham road, four miles to the east of Monkton Farleigh. St Michael's tower dates from the 1400s; however, the rest of the building was rebuilt early in the 19th-century.

Melksham
Map 1 ref C5
7 miles S of Chippenham on the A350

The busy market town of Melksham lies two miles southeast of Atworth at the junction of several major roads. William the Conqueror is said to have granted the original manor to Britric Aluric, a knight whose family name continues to be reflected in Melksham's renowned Aloeric School. Like Corsham and Trowbridge, the town grew into an important weaving centre during the 17th and 18th centuries, a period of prosperity which led to the building of some handsome merchants' houses around Canon Square.

Following the discovery of a chalybeate spring early in the 19th century, Melksham tried to reinvent itself as a spa town, and indeed a pump room was erected on the Devizes road which can still be seen today. However, the town was unable to compete with the much more fashionable Bath, and by 1822 the project was abandoned. Instead, Melksham turned to manufacturing and in 1819, the town was given a boost when a branch of the **Wiltshire and Berkshire Canal** was opened to link its many industrial concerns with the outside world. Although much changed, present-day Melksham retains an industrial feel in marked contrast to the rural gentility of many of its neighbours.

During medieval times, the once densely forested countryside around Melksham was an important royal hunting ground. Indeed, the area to the northeast of the town continues to be known as **Melksham Forest**, although over the years the trees have largely been cleared, first for agricultural use and then, as Melksham's industries continued to expand, for house building. Nevertheless, the area still offers some pleasant walking.

Situated a mile from the centre of Melksham off the A3102 Calne road, **Toxique** is an award-winning restaurant with exclusive accommodation which lies in the very heart of Wiltshire, yet is only fifteen minutes drive from junction 17 on the M4. This beautiful stone farmhouse has been converted into an outstanding establishment which is extensively recommended: the Good Food Guide named it County Restaurant of the Year 1994, the Which? Hotel Guide named it County Hotel of the Year 1996, and it is also acclaimed by Egon Ronay, the Michelin Guide, the AA Restaurant Guide, and the Ackerman Guide.

Hosts Peter Jewkes and Helen Bartlett have successfully created an atmosphere which is tasteful and stylish, yet warm and refreshingly informal. The food too is superb. On the evening we visited, the imaginative list of starters included seared squid with sweet peppers and coconut and lime soup, and the main courses included duck, venison, fillet steak, sea bass and red mullet. There was also a choice of mouthwatering desserts and fine wines to accompany the meal. As an impressive sideline, Toxique produces a range of hampers and food gift boxes which can be collected or delivered throughout the world.

For those wanting to stay, there are five individually-styled bed-room suites: the Oriental Suite is simple in design, with clean white walls and hanging drapes; the Rococo Suite, with its opulent feel, is in complete contrast, with deep rich reds and tartans adorning the walls and a large four-poster bed complete with dark drapes and gold accessories; the Colonial Suite is light, bright and airy, with traditional rattan chairs and wooden furniture; the Desert Suite is decorated throughout in muted shades of blue, yellow and gold; and the Moroccan Suite occupies the attic spaces with cushions scat-

Toxique Restaurant

tered on the floor, gold drapes round the bed, and a fabulous view from the bath. (It also has sloping ceilings which could be a problem for the very tall.) With its superb food, accommodation and surroundings, Toxique offers an experience unique in the UK. For lovers of fine seafood, Toxique has an equally stylish sister restaurant in North Parade, Bath (Tel: 01225 445983). *Toxique Restaurant, 187 Woodrow Road, Melksham, Wiltshire Tel: 01225 702129*

Great Chalfield
Map 1 ref B5

9 miles SW of Chippenham off the B3109

Three miles to the west of Melksham, a narrow country lane leads to **Great Chalfield Manor**, a superb Tudor manor house which was built by Thomas Tropenell in the 1480s. Now owned by the National Trust, this delightful moated residence is approached through an arched gateway and across a polished stone courtyard overlooked by oriel windows. Its many exceptional internal features include an original Tudor screen, an impressive great hall, and a dining room containing a portrait of the original owner, who was also responsible for constructing the bell tower and spire on the nearby 13th-century parish church. Great Chalfield Manor is lived in by the descendants of Major R Fuller who carried out substantial restoration work early in the 20th century. (Open for guided tours on Tuesdays, Wednesdays and Thursdays between 1 April and end-October.)

Holt
Map 1 ref C6

3 miles N of trowbridge on the B3107

Another National Trust-owned property, the **Courts Garden**, lies a mile and a half to the south of Great Chalfield near the village of Holt. The present-day house, which regrettably is not open to the public, was constructed in neo-Gothic style around 1800, although its elegant decorated facade dates from around a century earlier. It is so called because this was the place local weavers came to settle their disputes until the end of the 18th century. Around half of the beautiful seven-acre garden is arranged in formal style, with a lily pond, herbaceous borders and dividing yew hedges, and the remainder is a wild garden with an arboretum. (Open daily except Saturdays, 2pm to 5pm between late March and early November.)

Holt is a community of handsome 17th and 18th-century houses set around an attractive green on the B3107 Melksham to Bradford-on-Avon road. The village was once a small spa, and indeed the old mineral well can still be seen in the grounds of a local factory.

Bradford-on-Avon
Map 1 ref B6

3 miles NW of Trowbridge on the A363

The historic market town of Bradford-on-Avon is situated at an ancient bridging point on the River Avon, a couple of miles to the west. A settlement has stood on this important riverside site since the time of the Saxons. Indeed, the town's oldest building, the **Church of St Lawrence**, is believed to have been founded by St Aldhelm around 700 AD. Once part of a monastery which was largely destroyed by the Danes, the building *"disappeared"* for over a thousand years, during which time the townspeople used it as a school, a charnel house for storing the bones of the dead, and a residential dwelling.

The building was only rediscovered in 1858, when a clergyman looking down from the hill above the town spied the cruciform shape of a church. Further investigations on the site revealed two carved angels and confirmed the structure as the Saxon place of worship which had been *"missing"* for over ten centuries. The surrounding buildings were gradually removed to reveal the present gem which, at only 38ft long and with a chancel arch only three feet wide, is one of the smallest churches in the country. Bradford-on-Avon also boasts an attractive Norman church which was extensively restored in the 19th century. The interior contains a number of interesting memorials, including that of Lieutenant-General Henry Shrapnel, the army officer who in 1785 invented the shrapnel shell.

Perhaps the town's best known feature is the superb nine-arched bridge which spans the River Avon. Originally constructed in the 13th century for packhorse traffic, it was extensively rebuilt in the 17th century. The small, domed building near its southern end is a tiny former chapel which subsequently became the town lock-up. John Wesley is said to have spent an uncomfortable night here; however, the two cells were more often employed to house local drunks, a use which led to the building being dubbed the *"Blind House"*.

Another of Bradford's outstanding buildings, the **Tithe Barn**, dates from the time the town was under the administration of the nuns of Shaftesbury Abbey. By the 14th century, the increased output from the surrounding farms had created such a problem in storing the *"tithes"* - one tenth of the local farmers' annual produce - that a new storehouse had to be built near the river. The result was the gigantic tithe barn 164ft long and 33ft wide which had fourteen bays, four projecting porches and a roof consisting of 30,000 stone tiles weighing an estimated 100 tons. Today, this magnificent stone building houses an interesting collection of antique farm implements and agricultural machinery.

During the 16th and 17th centuries, Bradford-on-Avon stood at the heart of one of Britain's great sheep farming areas. As a result, it became a major centre of the wool industry and attracted skilled weavers from all over Europe. Indeed, so important was the town that it is even rumoured to have given Yorkshire's Bradford its name. Despite protests from local self-employed weavers the industry gradually became more mechanised, and by the early 1800s around thirty water-powered cloth-mills were operating in the locality. Within 100 years, however, the lack of a local coal supply forced them all to close as the industry transferred to the industrialised North.

The period of prosperity during the 16th and 17th centuries left Bradford-on Avon with a legacy of handsome old stone buildings, most notably **The Hall**, a fine early-Jacobean residence which was built by John Hall in 1610. Today, the grounds may be visited by appointment. Other historic attractions in the town include the **Priory**, **Westbury House**, and the **Shambles**, a unique early shopping precinct.

Westwood   *Map 1 ref B6*
3 miles W of Trowbridge off the A366

The attractive village of Westwood lies in the lanes off the B3109 Frome road, a mile and a half to the southwest of Bradford-on-Avon. This is site of the National Trust-owned **Westwood Manor**, a charming stone-built manor house which was constructed in the 15th century and then remodelled in the late 16th century. The interior contains a number of impressive period features, including some fine late Gothic windows and Jacobean plasterwork, and the grounds incorporate an interesting display of modern topiary. (Open Sundays, Tuesdays and Wednesdays, 2pm to 5pm between 1 April and 1 October.)

Another notable country house, **Iford Manor**, lies off the minor road to Freshford, a short distance to the northwest of Westwood. Although this handsome Tudor residence is not open to the public, its gardens are. Indeed, visitors come from all over the world to walk in the grounds which were laid out in Italian style by the landscape architect Harold Peto between 1898 and 1933. Said to have been inspired by Edwin Lutyens and Gertrude Jekyll, the layout makes imaginative use of the garden's idyllic setting beside the River Frome. The steeply sloping land behind the house has been fashioned into a series of delightful terraces which cascade with colour in early summer, and elsewhere, the ponds, statues and colonnades combine with the shrubs and trees to give the whole garden a wonderful romantic feel. (Open daily, except Fridays and non Bank Holiday Mondays, 2pm to 5pm between 1 May and 30 September; plus Sundays only in April and October.)

Iford Manor Gardens

Trowbridge   *Map 1 ref B6*

13 miles S of Chippenham on the A361

Trowbridge, the county town of Wiltshire, stands at an important
road junction, three miles to the east of Westwood. With roots going
back to the time of the Saxons, the present settlement grew up
around a Norman castle belonging to the de Bohun family, the curved
outline of which is indicated by the course of present-day Fore Street.
During the 17th and 18th centuries, Trowbridge grew into an important weaving centre and by 1830, as many as nineteen mills were
sited in the locality. An unusual number of handsome stone-built
townhouses dating from this period can still be seen in the heart of
the old town which is best explored on foot.

The parish church of St James was founded in 1483 by a wealthy
local cloth-maker on the site of an earlier Norman structure. Despite being further altered during the 19th century, it contains some

lavish decorations and is crowned by one of the finest parish church spires in the county. The chancel contains the tomb of former rector, George Crabbe, an acknowledged poet who was responsible for writing the work on which Benjamin Britten based his opera, Peter Grimes. By contrast, the grave of Thomas Helliber lies outside in the churchyard. Helliber was a local weaver who allegedly led a rebellion against the introduction of cloth-making machinery in 1803. Despite strongly proclaiming his innocence, he was convicted and hanged on the morning of his nineteenth birthday.

Another of Trowbridge's famous sons was Sir Isaac Pitman, the creator of the famous Pitman shorthand system who was born in a now-demolished house in Nash Yard in 1813. His links with the town are commemorated by a plaque and bust in the town hall, and in the naming of Pitman Avenue. The imaginatively presented **Trowbridge Museum** is situated in the Shires shopping centre in the heart of town. The museum tells the story of Trowbridge, its people and woollen industry using a series of reconstructed settings, including a weaver's cottage and a shearman's workshop. There is also a display of working textile machinery, cloth from which is on sale in the museum shop, and special collections of educational toys and children's games dating from the 18th century. (Open Tuesdays to Fridays 12 noon to 4pm, and Saturdays 10am to 5pm, all year round; admission free.)

Hilperton
Map 1 ref C6

1 mile NE of Trowbridge on the A361

Situated on the old A361 Devizes road two miles to the northeast of Trowbridge, the ancient village of Hilperton is mentioned in the

Lion and Fiddle

Domesday Book. This is the location of the **Lion and Fiddle**, an impressive free house set in two acres of land with lovely mature trees and ample parking which fronts onto the main road. An inn for over four centuries, it is thought to be the only licensed premises with this name in the country. The bar offers a choice of the finest English real ales, along with a range of snacks and light meals which are available at most times. Delicious homemade food is also served each day in the restaurant, supported by a selection of wines from around the world. There are also five en suite guest bedrooms which are nicely furnished and equipped with TVs and tea/coffee making facilities. Proprietor Henry Nurkowski provides a very friendly welcome and excellent hospitality. He is also delighted to discuss any requirements for special functions, be it a dinner party for two or a buffet for a hundred. *Lion and Fiddle, Hilperton, Near Trowbridge, Wiltshire Tel: 01225 776392*

Steeple Ashton
Map 1 ref C6

3 miles E of Trowbridge off the A350

The attractive village of Steeple Ashton lies in the country lanes, three miles to the east of Trowbridge. The long main street is lined with delightful old buildings, many of which are half-timbered and feature attractive red herringbone brickwork. There is also a strik-

Steeple Ashton

ing Norman village cross with four sundials. Perhaps the most striking feature, however, is the 15th-century parish church of **St Mary the Virgin** which, curiously enough, has been without a steeple since the original 93ft spire was destroyed by lightning in 1670. An impressive Perpendicular structure, the building contains some fine part-medieval stained-glass window lights and attractive lierne vaulting. It also houses the renowned **Samuel Hey Library** which numbers among its catalogue the early 15th-century Book of Hours, an illustrated Latin prayer book containing recommended worship for each hour of the day.

CHAPTER FIVE
North Wiltshire

Great Western Railway

5
North Wiltshire

Malmesbury
Map 1 ref C2
10 miles N of Chippenham on the A429

The old ecclesiastical centre of Malmesbury is a gem of a town which, thankfully, is bypassed by the main A429 Chippenham to Cirencester road. The oldest borough in England and still one of its most attractive places, this historic settlement stands around the site of an ancient hill fort on the southern margin of the Cotswolds. The Benedictine *Malmesbury Abbey* was founded here in the 7th century by St Aldhelm, then in 880 Alfred the Great granted the town a charter and so created what is perhaps the oldest borough in England.

In the 10th century, King Athelstan, Alfred's grandson and the first Saxon monarch to unite the whole of England, granted 500 acres of land to the townspeople of Malmesbury after they had helped him resist a Norse invasion. The area is still known as *King's Heath* and continues to be owned by around 200 residents of the town who can trace their ancestry back to the men who fought for the Saxon king over 1000 years ago. Athelstan made Malmesbury his capital in 925 and eventually was buried in the abbey in 941, an event which was properly recognised in the 15th century when an impressive monument was erected in his memory.

One of the first attempts at human-powered flight was made from the abbey tower by a monk from Malmesbury early in the 11th century. Brother Elmer (who is sometimes known as Oliver) strapped a pair of homemade wings to his arms, and flapping wildly, flew for some 200 yards before returning to earth, breaking both his legs in

Malmesbury Market Cross

the process and crippling himself for life. Despite this mishap, he lived on for another fifty years and is said to have predicted the Norman invasion following a sighting of Halley's comet. Elmer's pioneering flight is commemorated in one of the abbey's stained-glass windows.

Following Henry VIII's Dissolution of the Monasteries in 1539, Malmesbury Abbey was sold to a wealthy local wool merchant, William Stumpe, for the sum of £1,517 15s 2d. Stumpe proceeded to set up cloth-weaving workshops in the abbey buildings; however, the great church survived this indignity and was presented to the town as its new parish church in 1541. The remains of Malmesbury Abbey contain some outstanding Norman and Romanesque features, most notably the south porch with its ornately carved arch depicting scenes from the Bible, the ornate roof bosses in the nave, the 15th-century screen, and the *"watching loft"*. At one time, it possessed the oldest church organ in the country.

Malmesbury Abbey

The Old Bell Hotel, situated adjacent to the abbey, is thought to be one of the oldest hostelries in England. Established by an early Abbot of Malmesbury at a time when scholars came from all over Europe to study in the abbey's famous library, the inn was mentioned in the Domesday Book and is now a Grade I listed building. The reception hall contains a superb original fireplace, and one of the suites, the Athelstan, is named after Malmesbury's famous Saxon king.

Situated opposite the town car park in the centre of Malmesbury is **The Pottery**, a fascinating concern which is owned and run by a husband and wife team. A varied and unusual range of handmade ceramics is produced on site, in both stoneware and terra-cotta clays. Work on display includes decorative one-offs (look out for the renowned *"Malmesbury bowl"*), tableware, clocks, and wall and table lighting. Special commissions are also undertaken, including house names and numbers made to the customer's own specifications. *The Pottery, Cross Hayes, Malmesbury, Wiltshire Tel: 01666 825148*

The old part of Malmesbury lies between two branches of the Bristol Avon, and to reach its centre, it is necessary to cross one of six bridges and then climb the steep slope which leads to the market square. An unusual **Market Cross** stands in the centre of the square; an elaborate octagonal building with some fine vaulting, it was constructed in the late 15th century to provide shelter for the market traders.

The Whole Hog

An excellent place to call in for a relaxing drink, morning coffee, lunch or evening meal is the delightfully-named Whole Hog, an impressive pub and eating place which is situated in the centre of Malmesbury near the Market Cross. Sharon Jackson and her staff create a very congenial atmosphere which is welcoming to visitors and locals alike. The interior has been carefully refurbished, making clever use of floor to ceiling windows whilst retaining the building's traditional character and charm. Along with a warm welcome and friendly efficient service, customers are offered an impressive selection of real ales and a range of delicious food which is sure to suit all tastes. *The Whole Hog, 8 Market Cross, Malmesbury, Wiltshire   Tel: 01666 825845*

Other noteworthy buildings in the vicinity of Malmesbury's market square are the **Old Stone House**, with its handsome colonnade and grotesque gargoyles, the arched **Tolsey Gate**, whose two cells once served as the town gaol, and the **Abbey House** which was constructed by William Stumpe to replace the former abbot's residence. A stroll down the High Street leads past some lovely old buildings, most of which are constructed of locally-quarried stone.

The **Art Workshop** in the High Street is a fascinating place which provides everything for the working artist. Howard Wright offers a friendly and efficient bespoke framing service, and prides himself in being able to frame anything from paintings and prints, to tapestries and medals. He also stocks an extensive selection of materials for artists and craftspeople, with a special emphasis on those for calligraphy and silk painting. The Art Workshop is a delightful Aladdin's cave around which customers are welcome to browse. The unusually wide variety of materials on offer includes ranges of Cross and Shaeffer pens. *The Art Workshop, 53 High Street, Malmesbury, Wiltshire Tel: 01666 824755*

Whychurch Farm

Whychurch Farm is a working farm which is situated on the northern edge of Malmesbury. Ancient maps of the district show the area covered by the farm has been an important part of the local economy since the earliest times. The surrounding land was farmed by monks in the 11th and 12th-centuries, and one of the main farmhouse walls once formed part of the old church wall. Today, Mrs Weaver offers delightful bed and breakfast accommodation at the farmhouse and in two converted outbuildings, both of which have their own private entrances and en suite facilities.

All Whychurch Farm's accommodation is comfortable and beautifully presented. Breakfast is taken in the main house where Mrs Weaver keeps a wonderful collection of china, pottery and period furniture. Those who enjoy rummaging in antique and bric-a-brac shops will be in paradise here. A wide selection of items are for sale to visitors only, so prepare for a long and fascinating stay. A number inns and restaurants in the town and nearby villages are known for their excellent food. Whychurch Farm is situated near the road and has easy access and plenty of parking. Advance booking is recommended. *Whychurch Farm, Malmesbury, Wiltshire Tel: 01666 822156*

Garsdon
Map 1 ref D2

1 mile E of Malmesbury off the B4040

A minor road to the east of Malmesbury leads to Garsdon, a peaceful community whose church contains an unusual monument known as the **"Stars and Stripes"**. This distinctive tomb belongs to Laurence Washington, a local lord of the manor who was buried here in 1640, many years before the Stars and Stripes became a symbol of America. Washington bought the manor from Richard Moody, a contemporary of Henry VIII who is reputed to have been granted the estate as a reward for rescuing the king from a deep mud-filled mire after he had fallen from his horse. Early in the 20th century, the Stars and Stripes monument was restored with the help of funds donated by a number of American benefactors, including the Bishop of New York.

Charlton
Map 1 ref D2

2 miles NE of Malmesbury on the B4040

A mile to the north of Garsdon, the **Horse and Groom Inn** is a delightful pub and eating place which stands in a quintessentially English setting in the village of Charlton, two miles east of Malmesbury on the B4040 Cricklade road. This impressive 16th-century former coaching inn is owned and personally-run by Nichola and Philip, charming hosts who offer the finest food, ales and accommodation. Egon Ronay and AA recommended, the meals here are superb, with everything from the simplest bar snack to the most elaborate a la carte dish being freshly prepared to the highest standard. There are also three beautifully-decorated guest bedrooms

Horse and Groom Inn

available which are equipped with en suite bathrooms, direct-dial telephones, satellite TV and a number of thoughtful extras. *Horse and Groom Inn, Charlton, Near Malmesbury, Wiltshire Tel: 01666 823904 Fax: 01666 823390*

Oaksey   Map 1 ref D1
5 miles NE of Malmesbury off the A429
The country lanes to the northeast of Charlton lead through the villages of Hankerton and Eastcourt to the sprawling settlement of Oaksey. This attractive village contains some fine 17th-century cottages and a small 13th-century church which is renowned for its rare medieval murals. The south wall features an unusual painting entitled *"Christ of Trades"* which shows Jesus surrounded by an array of hand tools. No doubt, this served as a reminder to the congregation that the route to moral salvation lies through hard labour. The local lord of the manor, Lord Oaksey, is perhaps better known as John Oaksey, the former jockey and TV racing commentator. The interesting remains of the Norman motte and bailey fortification known as Norwood Castle lie on private land near Dean Farm to the north of the village.

Leigh   Map 2 ref E2
10 miles NE of Malmesbury off the B4696

For lovers of ancient English churches, the villages in the upper reaches of the Thames between Oaksey and Cricklade contain a couple of gems. The first can be found to the north of the B4040 Malmesbury to Cricklade road near the village of Leigh. Now disused, the **Church of All Saints** lies a quarter of a mile down a track from the Waterhay Bridge over the Thames. This lovely old building, which is also known as the Old Chancel, dates from the 12th century.

Ashton Keynes   Map 2 ref E1
10 miles NE of Malmesbury off the B4696

A couple of miles to the northwest, the **Church of the Holy Cross** stands on the edge of the sprawling village of Ashton Keynes. Also founded in the 12th century, the church was extended in the 13th century and extensively restored during the 1870s under the direction of William Butterfield, the architect of Keble College, Oxford. The farmyard adjoining the church is the site of a monastic house which was founded here in Saxon times. Both buildings are surrounded by the remnants of a double moat dating from before the Norman Invasion.

Ashton Keynes was once a manor belonging to King Alfred's sister, and it is still crisscrossed by hidden walkways which connect with the ancient church and inn. The village contains a number of fine old Cotswold-stone residences, including **Brook House** and **Ashton Mill**, and at one end of the village, the infant Thames runs beside the main street and the houses are reached by crossing one of the series of attractive small footbridges.

The ancient cross in the centre of the churchyard is one of Ashton Keynes' famous *"preaching crosses"*. All four were damaged during the English Civil War, although this one was restored as a war memorial in 1917. The churchyard also contains a number of table tombs belonging to the Richmond family, the local lords of the manor who lived at Cove House in the centre of Ashton Keynes. During the Civil War, the family's allegiances were tragically divided, with the sons choosing to fight on opposing sides. During a nighttime skirmish outside Ashton Keynes, one brother is reported to have unwittingly killed another, and when faced with the truth, he was so full of remorse that he took off for America and never returned. Ashton Keynes lies on the southern edge of the Cotswold Water Park.

Easton Grey   *Map 1 ref C2*
3 miles W of Malmesbury on the B4040

To the west of Malmesbury, a number of charming villages lie on either side of the B4040 Chipping Sodbury road. At Easton Grey, the southern branch of the River Avon is spanned by a handsome 16th-century bridge which has five low stone arches. As the curved main street rises from the riverbank it is lined with densely-packed grey limestone houses, most of which have mullioned windows and steeply-pitched gabled roofs.

A manor house has looked down from the hill above Easton Grey since the 13th century. The present building has a classical facade with an elegant covered portico which dates from the early 18th century. The beautiful landscaped grounds contain a small church with a fine Norman tower and font, and an interior which was extensively renovated during the 1830s. At one time, the house was used a summer retreat by Herbert Asquith, Britain's prime minister from 1908-16, and in 1923, it was occupied by the Prince of Wales during the Duke of Beaufort's hunting season at Badminton.

Sherston   *Map 1 ref B2*
4 miles W of Malmesbury on the B4040

The village of Sherston lies on the southern side of the B4040, two miles further west. Sometimes referred to by its historic name of Sherston Magna, this ancient settlement is arranged around the delightfully-named Rattlebone Inn, a hostelry with a long and interesting history. In 1016, Edmund Ironside defeated Canute near here in the Battle of Sherston and John Rattlebone, a local champion, sustained a mortal wound and breathed his last on the site now occupied by the inn. Another lovely old village, Sopworth, can be found in the lanes to the west of Sherston.

Stanton St Quintin   *Map 1 ref C3*
6 miles S of Malmesbury off the A429

The attractive community of Stanton St Quintin lies to the south of Malmesbury, within a mile of junction 17 on the M4. This surprisingly peaceful village is worth visiting for its exceptionally fine 11th-century **Church of St Giles**. Despite being altered in the 15th century and again by the Victorians, its unusual 12th-century carved figure of the enthroned Christ with a dragon at his feet has been left untouched outside under the west window. Excellent bed and breakfast accommodation is available at Stanton St Quintin's elegant former rectory, Stanton Court.

Biddestone

Map 1 ref B4

3 miles W of Chippenham off the A420

The lovely old village of Biddestone lies in the lanes a mile to the west of Sheldon Manor. An attractive settlement of stylish 17th and 18th-century houses set around a village green, its noteworthy buildings include a handsome gabled farmhouse with a Georgian gazebo which stands near the duck pond, and a grey stone manor house with a large walled garden which can be found on the edge of the village.

Situated between Sheldon and Biddestone Manors one mile from the picturesque village of Biddestone, the **Starfall Pottery** is a fascinating place to spend a few hours. Visitors to the studio can see the beautiful and skilled work of Gordon and Dorothy Whittle, two delightful people who extend a warm welcome at all times. As well as being superbly skilled at throwing pots, Gordon and Dorothy are equally proficient at decorating their work. Visitors are invited to observe the pottery-making process and view the wide and constantly-changing range of completed domestic stoneware, which includes a selection of individual commemorative pottery for christenings, weddings and other special occasions.

Starfall Pottery

There is also a display of non-pottery items produced by Dorothy, including those made from hand-spun, natural dyed wool, along with an assortment of unusual handmade cards and candles. All articles on display are for sale at very affordable prices, or if a special item is required, it can usually be made to order. Gordon and Dorothy also grow and sell a wide range of herb plants. They are extremely knowledgeable on the subject and are happy to give advice on the best plants to choose. The Starfall Pottery is open every day from 9am until dusk, all year round. *Starfall Pottery, Sheldon, Near Biddestone, Chippenham, Wiltshire Tel: 01249 713292*

Elaine Sexton provides a warm welcome at her delightful bed and breakfast establishment, **Elm Farm House**. Situated by Biddestone's village green, this picturesque 18th-century farmhouse has a half-acre walled garden, stables and direct access to its own fields and footpaths. Bedrooms are either en suite or with private bathroom, and are equipped TV and drinks facilities. A charming place to stay, Elm Farm House is English Tourist Board 2 crown commended. *Elm Farm House, The Green, Biddestone, Near Chippenham, Wiltshire Tel: 01249 713354*

Home Farm is a traditional family-owned and run farm of 200 acres which has a dairy herd, beef cattle and arable land. Set in a large and beautiful garden, this picture book 17th-century farmhouse is fronted by a half-acre paddock leading to the centre of Biddestone, where the two pubs both serve excellent meals. Ideal for children, guests are sure to enjoy the relaxed atmosphere and may come and go as they please. The bedrooms have private facilities and televisions, and a choice of breakfast is provided. With its good off-road parking and delightful location, Home Farm is ideal for touring the Cotswolds and Bath. *Home Farm, Harts Lane, Biddestone, Near Chippenham, Wiltshire Tel: 01249 714475*

Yatton Keynell
Map 1 ref B4

3 miles NW of Chippenham on the B4039

Two miles to the north of Biddestone in the village of Yatton Keynell, two fine old buildings stand at the heart of the community, the **Bell Inn** and the 15th-century **Church of St Margaret of Antioch**. Part of the church was built as a shrine by local landowner Sir William Keynell to show his gratitude to God for protecting him in battle and returning him safely to England from the Crusades. The Bell was originally constructed as a farmhouse during the 1400s and only became an inn in the 18th century because of its close proximity to what was then the main coaching route between Bristol, Chippenham and London. An unusual fertility stone was discovered here during renovation work, although evidently, it had not been in use for many years as the population of the village remains very small!

Castle Combe

Map 1 ref B4

5 miles NW of Chippenham on the B4039

From Yatton Keynell, it is only a short drive northwest to Castle Combe, one of the loveliest villages in the southern Cotswolds. Indeed in 1962, Castle Combe was named the *"prettiest village in England"*, a factor which led to it becoming a location for the film, Doctor Doolittle. Several decades of exposure has placed the village well and truly on the tourist map. However, during the 15th and 16th centuries, it earned its living as a cloth-weaving centre. Many of the present-day buildings date from this period, including the Perpendicular church of St Andrew with its fine fan vaulting, 13th-century font and memorial to Walter Dunstanville, the founder of the now-demolished castle from which the village takes its name.

Castle Combe lies in a deep, tree-lined valley and visitors are encouraged to park their cars at the top and walk down through the narrow streets. One of the finest views of the old village can be had by looking back up the hill from the picturesque three-arched bridge over the By Brook, also a good viewpoint for spotting trout. Among the many impressive buildings to be seen here are the 15th-century covered market cross, the site of a once-regular wool market, and the 16th-century manor house, a building which was much altered

Alicia Cottage

during the Victorian period and is now a hotel. In marked contrast with the rest of the village, Castle Combe also has a famous motor racing circuit which is located beside the B4039, three-quarters of a mile to the east.

Alicia Cottage is an outstanding bed and breakfast establishment which is situated in the heart of Castle Combe, within easy reach of historic Bath and the beautiful Cotswolds. The discerning traveller will certainly enjoy this charming 300 year-old Cotswold stone cottage which is the lovely home of Doreen Sanders. The house is centrally heated and very tastefully furnished, and guests have their own dining room and a drawing room with an open log fire. Bedrooms have private facilities en suite, and in the morning there is the choice of either an English or continental breakfast. At Alicia Cottage, guests are able to experience life in genuine rural surroundings, with lovely walks through picturesque valleys. The cottage has parking available, but is unsuitable for smokers. *Alicia Cottage, School Lane, Castle Combe, Near Chippenham, Wiltshire Tel: 01249 782110*

Swindon *Map 2 ref F2/3*

Swindon, the largest town in Wiltshire, lies in the northeast corner of the county between the Cotswolds and the Marlborough Downs. An important commercial centre which enjoys direct access to the busy M4 corridor, before the ***Great Western Railway's*** main London to Bristol line was completed in 1835, it was a sleepy community whose principal activity was agriculture. Swindon station was opened in that year, although it wasn't until some time later that the GWR's principal engineer, Isambard Kingdom Brunel, made the decision which was to change the town out of all recognition.

Legend has it that one day, Brunel was attempting to solve the problem of where to locate the company's main railway workshops whilst walking along the Swindon stretch of line. Apparently, he found the question so exasperating that he finally threw his half-finished sandwich into the air and shouted, *"wherever it lands, there shall I build".*

Construction got underway shortly after and within a few years, Swindon locomotive works had grown to become one of the largest railway workshops in the world. At one time, 12,000 workers were employed on the 320-acre site which incorporated the *"Railway Village"*, a model development of 300 artisan's homes which were built in limestone extracted from ***Box Tunnel*** near Bath. Today, this unique example of Victorian town planning is open to the public as

Great Western Railway Museum, Swindon

a living museum. One of its most interesting exhibits is a railway foreman's house of 1842 which is furnished in the style of the period. (Open daily, 10am to 1pm (not Sundays) and 2pm to 5pm, all year round.)

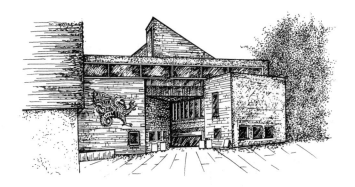

Wyvern Theatre and Arts Centre, Swindon

The site in Faringdon Road also contains the world famous Great Western Railway Museum. Situated in one of the former workers' hostels or *"navvies' barracks"*, the museum houses a fascinating collection of steam locomotives, signalling equipment, railway signs and other GWR railwayana, and includes a special room devoted to the life and achievements of Isambard Kingdom Brunel. (Open daily, 10am (2pm Sundays) to 5pm, all year round.)
Present-day Swindon is a bustling commercial town which at one time was the fastest growing centre of population in Europe. Re-

Brunel Shopping Centre, Swindon

gent Street and the **Brunel Centre** offer some excellent shopping facilities, and the town is well catered for in the area of arts and entertainment. The Wyvern Theatre is a luxury 650-seat venue which stages everything from rock concerts to large-scale touring theatre and ballet productions, and both the Arts Centre and the Link Arts Studio have 200-seat auditoriums which provide a more intimate atmosphere for dance, drama and performance arts.

Swindon's renowned Art Gallery in Bath Road features work by such acclaimed modern artists as Ben Nicholson, Graham Sutherland and L S Lowry (open 10am to 6pm on Mondays to Saturdays and 2pm to 5pm on Sundays, all year round), and the town also contains a number of beautifully-kept parks and open spaces, including Queen's Park, Penhill Park and Faringdon Road Park, part of the GWR's original Railway Village development.

The busy A419 to the northwest of Swindon follows the course of Ermin Street, the great Roman road which linked the garrison towns of Glevum (Gloucester) and Calleva (Silchester) in Hampshire. This ancient thoroughfare followed a virtually straight course for most of its sixty-mile length, a characteristic which is clearly demonstrated in the section between Swindon and Cirencester.

Blunsdon   Map 2 ref F2
2 miles N of Swindon on the A419

The pleasant community of Blunsdon St Andrew lies to the west of this road, three miles from Swindon town centre. The ruins which can be seen beside the tiny 13th-century church are the remains of **Blunsdon Abbey**, a once-impressive monastic house which burnt to the ground many years ago. The abbey grounds now contain a pleasant caravan and camping park. Blunsdon St Andrew's sister village of Broad Blunsdon lies on the eastern side of the A419. This historic village possesses a fine Early English church which is linked by a pathway to Castle Hill, the site of a pre-Roman earthwork fortification.

Cricklade   Map 2 ref E1
6 miles N of Swindon off the A419

The attractive small town of Cricklade lies a little to the west of the A419 Ermin Street, four miles northwest of Broad Blunsdon. An ancient settlement with a history stretching back beyond the days of the Roman occupation, a mint was located here during Saxon times. Several centuries later, the Normans founded the town's principal church which they dedicated to St Sampson, a Breton saint born in 465. The main structure was built between the 12th and

15th centuries, and the magnificent cathedral-like tower was added by the Duke of Northumberland in the Tudor period around 1550. Along with some fine Norman detailing, the interior contains a number of rare heraldic carvings and an unusual Elizabethan altar table. St Sampson's is now the principal venue for Cricklade's widely-renowned annual Festival of Music which is held in the town in September.

The smaller church of St Mary can be found at the opposite end of the High Street near the remains of Cricklade's 13th-century priory and hospital. The priory has now been converted into attractive small residential dwellings. Also worth seeing is the famous school which was founded by London goldsmith, Robert Jenner, in 1651. A good way to find out more about Cricklade's long and interesting history is to visit the small museum which is situated opposite the clock tower in Calcutt Street. (Open Wednesdays 2pm to 4pm and Saturdays 10am to 12 noon.)

For those interested in industrial archeology it is worth finding **West Mill Wharf** in West Mill Lane. This once-lively quay served the North Wiltshire branch of the **Wiltshire & Berkshire Canal**, and although now almost completely filled in, it serves as a poignant reminder of the golden age of Britain's inland waterways.

Cricklade is the only town in Wiltshire to lie on the River Thames, although at this point it could be better be described as a wide stream. The river flows under a bridge at the northern end of the High Street and from here, a well-worn footpath leads to **North Meadow**, an ancient water meadow which is home to some exceptionally rare plants and flowers. Designated a nature reserve in 1973, this unusual natural habitat a particular delight to behold in late-spring and summer. The pathway continues upstream to a footbridge, allowing the return journey to be made on the opposite bank of the Thames.

Latton   *Map 2 ref E1*
7 miles N of swindon on the A419

The lovely old village of Latton lies on the A419 Cirencester road, a mile to the northwest of Cricklade. A pleasant community which was originally part of an estate belonging to the Earl of St Germans, in more recent times it has been brought under the ownership of the Cooperative Wholesale Society who use it to house their agricultural workers, white collar staff and retired employees. Though relatively modest, the village possesses some delightful 17th-century Cotswold stone cottages and larger Victorian houses. The part-Norman church was substantially rebuilt by the forthright Victorian architect, William Butterfield.

Latton once stood at an important junction of the **Wiltshire & Berkshire** and **Thames & Severn** canals, and **Latton Basin**, a busy holding area where barges used to manoeuvre and wait, can still be made out in the old canal bed. The footpath which follows the course of the canal to the northwest leads to the remains of a disused lock, next to which can be seen a curious round lock-keeper's house. An impressive old wharf owner's (or wharfinger's) house with an imposing classical pediment appears somewhat out of place when viewed from the main A419 between Latton and Cricklade.

Marston Meysey   Map 2 ref F1
7 miles N of Swindon off the A419

The delightfully-named community of Marston Meysey lies on the northern bank of the Thames, a mile and a half to the northeast of Latton. The northernmost village in Wiltshire, its long main street is lined with handsome old houses and cottages. A bridge crosses the North Wiltshire branch of the Wiltshire and Berkshire Canal on the edge of the village, and near here, an unusual canal lock-keeper's roundhouse can be seen which is similar to the one at Latton.

Highworth   Map 2 ref F2
5 miles NE of Swindon on the A361

On the northeastern side of Swindon, the aptly-named small town of Highworth stands at the top of a 400ft incline on the A361 midway between Swindon and Lechlade. This pleasant community contains some exceptional 17th and 18th-century domestic architectural, examples of which can be found around the old square in the town centre. Noteworthy buildings from this period include **Highworth House** and **Jesmond House**, now a hotel.

Highworth parish church was built in Perpendicular style during the 15th century. The structure was fortified during the English Civil War and shortly after, it was attacked by Parliamentarian forces under Fairfax. One of the cannon balls which struck the building is now on display inside. There is also a memorial to a Lieutenant Warneford who was awarded the Victoria Cross for destroying the first enemy Zeppelin in 1915. A pleasant walk leads up from the town to the summit of the Highworth Hill. The magnificent view from here takes in the counties of Wiltshire, Gloucestershire and Oxfordshire. Further north, the land slopes gradually down towards the gently-rolling valley of the upper Thames.

Sevenhampton
Map 2 ref F2
5 miles NE of Swindon off the A361

At Sevenhampton, between the A361 and A420 a mile to the south of Highworth, **Roves Farm Visitor Centre** offers an interesting afternoon out on a working livestock farm. Visitors can meet Gladys the pig and her friends, including lambs, calves, goats, rabbits and ducks. They can also take a guided trailer ride around farm, try their hand at spinning and weaving, have fun on the adventure playground, or enjoy a delicious cream tea. (Open Wednesday to Sundays, 11am to 5pm between March and end-September.) At Wanborough, on the southeastern edge of Swindon, Lotmead Farm offers top quality pick-your-own soft fruit and vegetables between early June and October.

Bishopstone
Map 2 ref G3
3 miles E of Swindon off the B4000

Three miles further east, the peaceful downland village of Bishopstone lies in a dramatic position beneath the ridge of the Bishopstone Downs. This is the location of **Cheney Thatch**, an outstanding bed and breakfast establishment which could be the model for all those delightful thatched cottage picture postcards.

Cheney Thatch

The home of John and Rosemary Boot, this superb country cottage has its own heated swimming pool and is the perfect place to stay for those wanting first-class accommodation and a marvellous English breakfast. The beautiful surrounding countryside contains an abundance of wildlife, including trout, doves, ducks, waterfowl and a wide variety of wild birds. Cheney Thatch lies only four miles from junction 15 on the M4 and is situated within easy driving distance of Bath, Bristol, London and the Cotswolds. It provides the perfect base for those wanting peaceful and luxurious surroundings while touring southern England. Advance booking strongly recommended. *Cheney Thatch, Bishopstone, Near Swindon, Wiltshire Tel: 01793 790508*

Liddington
Map 2 ref F3

3 miles SE of Swindon on the B4192

The landscape to the south of Swindon is very different to that to the north. Here, the land rises dramatically onto the exposed plateau of the Marlborough Downs. The main A345 Swindon to Marlborough road leads into the heart of this scenic expanse of countryside, and to the east of this road, the remains of **Liddington Castle** can be seen on the ridge above junction 15 on the M4. This impressive Iron Age hill fort occupies a seven-acre site on a high down whose summit is over 900ft above sea level. The structure consists of a series of wide ditches and earthwork ramparts which offer some magnificent views over the Vale of the White Horse to the distant Cotswold Hills.

Ogbourne St George
Map 2 ref F4

6 miles S of Swindon off the A345

Ogbourne St George, the largest and most northerly of the three villages known collectively as the Ogbournes, is an ancient settlement which lies off the A345, four miles south of Liddington Castle. The village has Saxon roots and is mentioned in the Domesday Book. Its delightful 12th-century church stands just below the **Ridgeway Path**, the famous long-distance footpath which runs for over seventy miles from the ancient settlements of the Kennet Valley in Wiltshire to Ivinghoe on the Buckinghamshire-Bedfordshire border. One of Europe's oldest routes, the Ridgeway makes a dramatic curve at this point, almost surrounding the village on three sides.

A pleasant four-mile walk along the Ridgeway to the west of Ogbourne St George leads along **Burderop Down** to the site of the Iron Age stronghold, **Barbury Castle**, one of the most spectacular and widely-visited hill forts in southern England. (It can also be reached by road from the north via Wroughton or Chiseldon.) This clearly-defined twelve-acre site is surrounded by a double line of earthwork ramparts which are breached to the east and west by narrow entrances.

The view over the surrounding downland landscape from the perimeter rim is breathtaking. The outline of an Iron Age field system can just be made out to the east, and half a mile to the north, the open hillside is noted for being the scene of a bloody battle between the Britons and the Saxons in the 6th century. This ended in defeat for the Britons and established a Saxon kingdom of Wessex under King Ceawlin. The whole area has now been designated the Barbury Castle Country Park.

Aldbourne   *Map 2 ref G4*
6 miles SE of Swindon on the B4192
A minor road to the east of Ogbourne St George leads to the picturesque village of Aldbourne. Set 700ft up in the Marlborough Downs, this attractive community has all the ingredients of a quintessential English village. There is a charming village green with a duck pond and weathered stone cross, a 15th-century parish church containing a superbly-carved alabaster monument to a priest, a 16th-century court house, and a square surrounded by ancient cottages and Georgian houses. In the 17th and 18th centuries, Aldbourne was renowned for its bell founding, millinery and cloth-weaving; today, it is a quiet place which regularly wins the award for best-kept village in Wiltshire.

Ramsbury   *Map 2 ref G4*
8 miles SE of Swindon off the B4192
To the southeast of Aldbourne, the B4192 Hungerford road descends into the valley of the River Kennet. The once important ecclesiastical centre of Ramsbury can be found on the northern side of the river, a mile to the west of the main road. Between the years 909 and 1058, this tranquil spot was a residence of the Bishops of Wiltshire. The 13th-century parish church was built on the foundations of a much-earlier building dating from the time of the Saxon bishops.

Present-day Ramsbury contains a number of attractive Jacobean and Georgian buildings, many of which have gardens running down to the River Kennet. The oak tree in the square was planted by a building society in 1986 to replace a mature oak which they had used as a logo. The removal of the old tree caused a certain amount of controversy however, for according to village legend, it was the home of the local witch, Maud Toogood. Just outside Ramsbury, the River Kennet borders the grounds of the impressive Ramsbury Manor, a private house which was built in 1680 by Inigo Jones' pupil and son-in-law, John Webb.

Chilton Foliat   Map 2 ref H5
9 miles SE of Swindon on the B4192

Three miles downstream from Ramsbury, the B4192 crosses the River Kennet near the village of Chilton Foliat, a pleasant community of old timber-framed cottages and Georgian residential buildings whose 13th-century church is constructed of flint and stone. After crossing the bridge, a minor road to the southwest of Chilton Foliat leads to **Littlecote House**, a Tudor mansion which was built between 1490 and 1520 on the site of a medieval manor. Some of the earliest visitors to this fine gabled house were Henry VIII and Jane Seymour whose entwined initials can be seen in a stained-glass window in the great hall, confirmation that some of their early encounters took place here.

Littlecote's most notorious occupant, however, was *"Wild Darrell"*, the owner who constructed the magnificent 110ft Long Gallery. Darrell is thought to have been responsible for making one of his resident ladies-in-waiting pregnant; then after she had given birth, he is alleged to have taken the newborn baby and thrown it onto the fire. Legend has it that the house has been haunted ever since, both by the spirit of the screaming infant and by the ghost of its mother who wanders the corridors looking for her lost child.

In 1589, the Littlecote House was acquired by Sir John Popham, a lawyer who went on to become the Lord Chief Justice. An original set of finger stocks which were used to restrain those appearing before him can be seen in the great hall. During the English Civil War, his grandson, Colonel Alexander Popham, commanded a Parliamentarian force known as the Littlecote Garrison. A fine collection of arms and uniforms from the period are on display in the house.

Littlecote House stands in a wonderful position on the banks of the River Kennet. The site has been occupied since Roman times, and indeed a **Roman Villa** was built here around 170 AD to which an elaborate floor mosaic was added over 100 years later. This was first discovered in the 18th century; however, to prevent its likely destruction, it was reburied under tons of earth where it remained undisturbed until 1977. Now fully excavated, the three-acre villa site forms one of Littlecote's main attractions. Others include the Puritan chapel, stream railway, children's adventure playground and spectacular demonstrations of falconry and medieval jousting. (Open daily, 10am to 6pm between March and end-September.)

Wroughton Map 2 ref F3
3 miles S of Swindon on the A4361

A number of interesting places can be found in the foothills of the Marlborough Downs to the southwest of Swindon. Wroughton is the home of a highly-regarded **Science Museum** which is housed

National Air Transport Collection, Wroughton

in a series of refurbished aircraft hangars on its former airfield.

The national collection of civil and commercial aircraft is located here, along with a selection of historic space rockets, hovercraft, fire-fighting appliances and aero and marine engines. One hangar is devoted to vintage buses, steam and motor lorries, historic cars, motorbikes and bicycles, and another houses a collection of early farm machinery and agricultural implements. A number of specialist air shows and rallies are held here throughout the year, including the International Kite Festival in May and the Jet World Masters in August. The nearby **Butser Ancient Farm Project** and **Clauts Wood Nature Reserve** are two further attractions which are worth a visit.

Situated in Wroughton's main street and conveniently-located for Swindon and the M4, Rosemary Allen provides first-rate bed and breakfast accommodation at **Hollyhocks Cottage**. Guests have to be a little nimble to climb the stairs, but it's all part of the charm of this delightful cottage home. There are a number of good pubs locally, and the cottage is handy for the local air and motor museum. *Hollyhocks Cottage, 15 High Street, Wroughton, Near Swindon, Wiltshire Tel: 01793 813455*

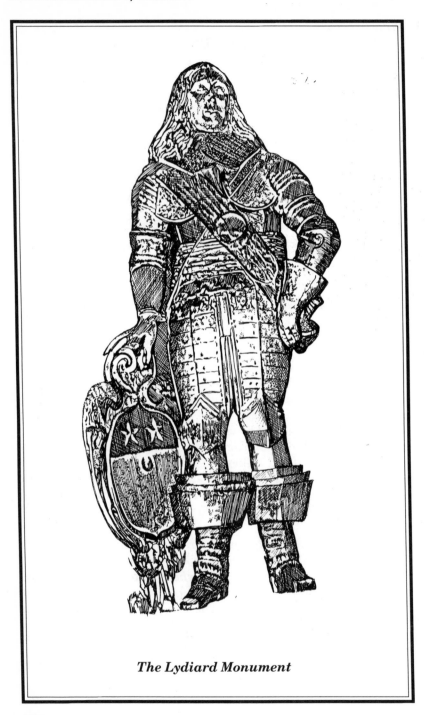

The Lydiard Monument

Wootton Bassett
Map 2 ref E3

3 miles W of Swindon off the A3102

Five miles to the west of Wroughton, the small dormitory town of
Wootton Bassett is situated on the A3102, close to its junction with
the M4. This bustling community contains a number of fine historic
buildings including the **Old Town Hall**, an unusual structure which
stands on a series of tall stone piers. The open-sided ground-floor
area once served as a covered market and still provides shelter for
the old town stocks. The upper floor, which contained the former
town chambers, now houses an interesting museum of local history.

Lydiard Tregoze
Map 2 ref E2

2 miles W of Swindon off the A3102

A couple of miles to the north, the lanes on the western side of Swindon contain some attractive old villages. Sounding as if it would be
more at home in Cornwall, the settlement of Lydiard Tregoze originally grew up around an old Saxon manor house. However, alterations made during the 18th-century when the fashion for emparking
was at its height required the manorial estate *"be free from unsightly
buildings"* and so the village was progressively dismantled. The
only original structure of significance to survive is the medieval
church of St Mary, a lovely little building with an unusually bright

Lydiard Park

and colourful interior. Its most striking feature, a monument known
as the **Golden Cavalier**, is a full-size gilded effigy of Edward St
John who was killed at the second Battle of Newbury in 1645. Other
attractions include the early-17th-century pulpit, some striking 15th-
century stained glass, a cabinet containing a brightly coloured trip-
tych, and the St John family pew.

The distinguished St John family, one 15th-century member of which was the grandmother of the first Tudor monarch Henry VII, lived at nearby Lydiard Park, a magnificent country mansion which is now under the ownership of Thamesdown Borough Council. The original medieval manor house was replaced in 1745 by the present building, which has a splendid neoclassical pedimented facade and rococo interior. The house has been extensively restored and is now furnished with fine paintings and elegant Georgian furniture. The mansion is the central attraction in the 260-acre Lydiard Park estate, an attractive area of open lawns and woodland which incorporates a visitor centre with an exhibition on local natural history, and a children's adventure play area with a full-size western fort.

Purton   *Map 2 ref E2*
3 miles NW of Swindon off the B4553

Purton, a mile and a half to the north, is a long sprawling community with a fine part-Norman church, one of only a handful in England to possess both a tower and a spire. According to local legend, the church ended up with two towers after the two sisters who originally commissioned the building were unable to agree upon a single design. (It turns out, however, that the structures were built 150 years apart, the central tower with its spire having been constructed around 1325 and the western pinnacled tower around 1475.) Although much altered, evidence of the church's Norman origins can be seen in the architectural detailing. The windows incorporate some rare fragments of medieval stained-glass, and the interior contains a number of striking murals, including a 17th-century interpretation of the Death of the Virgin.

The elegant Cotswold stone hotel of Francis and Anne Young lies nestled in the Vale of the White Horse between the Cotswolds and Marlborough Downs. Once the local vicarage, the **Pear Tree** at Church End is set in seven and a half acres of beautiful grounds on the outskirts of Purton. The RAC has awarded the establishment its highest award for excellence - the Blue Ribbon - whilst the AA have given it a 3 star rating with 2 restaurant rosettes; it is further acclaimed by Egon Ronay and the Good Hotel Guide.

The Conservatory Restaurant is the perfect setting in which to enjoy chef Catherine Berry's superb and imaginative cuisine. Based on modern English cooking, she uses only the finest fresh ingredients and herbs from the hotel's own extensive garden. Each of the eighteen superb, individually-decorated rooms and suites is named after a character associated with Purton, for example Ann Hyde,

The Pear Tree

the mother of Queen Mary, and Neville Maskelyne, the Astronomer Royal. Lying only minutes away from the M4, this peaceful and luxurious English country hotel is situated within easy driving distance of Cirencester, Bath, Oxford, Avebury, Stonehenge and the Cotswold villages. *The Pear Tree, Church End, Purton, Near Swindon, Wiltshire Tel: 01793 772100 Fax: 01793 772369*

A mile to the north of Purton, a bend in the road known as Watkins' Corner is named after a man who was hanged here for a murder. According to local lore, as Watkins swung from the gallows rope a sudden squall blew up, causing the hangman's horse to bolt. The startled animal threw the hangman to the ground, breaking his neck and killing him outright. Some time after, it emerged the murder had actually been committed by Watkins' father, and to this day, this lonely place is said to be haunted by the spirit of the unjustly condemned man.

Tourist Information Centres

Centres in bold are open all the year around.

Amesbury Tourist Information Centre
  Redworth House, Flower Lane, Amesbury, Wiltshire, SP4 7HG
  Tel No: 01980 622833

Avebury Tourist Information Centre
  The Great Barn, Avebury, Wiltshire, SN8 1RF
  Tel No: 01672 539425

Bradford on Avon Tourist Information Centre
  34 Silver Street, Bradford on Avon, Wiltshire, BA15 1JX
  Tel No: 01225 865797

Chippenham Tourist Information Centre
  The Citadel, Bath Road, Chippenham, Wiltshire, SN15 2AA
  Tel No: 01249 657733

Devizes Tourist Information Centre
  39 St John's Street, Devizes, Wiltshire, SN10 1BL
  Tel No: 01380 729408

Malmesbury Tourist Information Centre
  Town Hall, Market Lane, Malmesbury, Wiltshire, SN16 9BZ
  Tel No: 01666 823748

Marlborough Tourist Information Centre
  Car Park, George Lane, Marlborough, Wiltshire, SN8 1EE
  Tel No: 01672 513989

Melksham Tourist Information Centre
Church Street, Melksham, Wiltshire, SN12 6LS
Tel No: 01225 707424

Mere Tourist Information Centre
The Square, Mere, Wiltshire, BA12 6JJ
Tel No: 01747 861211

Salisbury Tourist Information Centre
Fish Row, Salisbury, Wiltshire, SP1 1EJ
Tel No: 01722 334956

Swindon Tourist Information Centre
37 Regent Street, Swindon, Wiltshire, SN1 1JL
Tel No: 01793 530328

Trowbridge Tourist Information Centre
St Stephen's Place, Trowbridge, Wiltshire, BA14 8AH
Tel No: 01225 777054

Warminster Tourist Information Centre
Central Car Park, Warminster, Wiltshire, BA12 9BT
Tel No: 01985 218548

Westbury Tourist Information Centre
The Library, Edward Street, Westbury, Wiltshire, BA13 3BD
Tel No: 01373 827158

Index

N

Netherhampton   22
Netton   27
Newhouse, Redlynch   18
Nine Men's Morris, Berwick St
      James   24
North Meadow, Cricklade   129
Nunton   16
Nunton House, Nunton   16

O

Oaksey   119
Odstock   16
Ogbourne St George   132
Old Market Hall, Mere   43
Old Sarum, Salisbury   3
Old Stone House,
      Malmesbury   117
Old Town Hall, Wooton
      Bassett   137
Old Wardour Castle, Ansty   48
Oldbury Castle, Cherhill   89
Oxford and the South Wiltshire
      Museum, Salisbury   45

P

Pepperbox Hill, Lover   18
Pewsey   60
Philipps House, Dinton   23
Place Farm, Tisbury   49
Porch House, Potterne   77
Porton Down, Stratford-sub-
      Castle   26
Potterne   77
Poultry Cross, Salisbury   9
Priory, Bradford-on-Avon   106
Purton   138
Pyt House, Tisbury   49

Q

Queensbury Bridge, West
      Amesbury   27

R

Ramsbury   133
Redlynch   18
Ridgeway Long Distance Footpath,
      West Overton   63
Ridgeway Path, Ogbourne St
      George   132
Roman villa, Chilton Foliat   134
Roundway Hill, Bishops
      Cannings   71
Roves Farm Visitor Centre,
      Sevenhampton   131
Rybury, Alton Barnes   62

S

, Salisbury   80
Salisbury   3
Salisbury and South Wiltshire
      Museum, Salisbury   6
Salisbury Cathedral, Salisbury   3
Salisbury Plain   80
Salisbury Racecourse   23
Samuel Hey Library, Steeple
      Ashton   110
Sandy Lane   90
Sarum, Old   25
Savernake   54
Savernake Forest, Savernake   54
Saxon Church, Britford   15
Science Museum, Wroughton   135
Sevenhampton   131
Shaftesbury   44
Shambles, Bradford-on-Avon   106
Sheldon Manor, Chippenham   87
Sherston   121
Silbury Hill   64
Somerset Hospital, Froxfield   58
St Cyriacs Church, Lacock   93
St John the Baptist's church,
      Horningsham   40
St Mary the Virgin, Steeple
      Ashton   109
Stanton St Quintin   121
Stars and Stripes, Garsdon   118
Steeple Ashton   109
Stockton   39

The Hidden Places Series

ORDER FORM

To order more copies of this title or any of the others in this series
please complete the order form below and send to:

**Travel Publishing Ltd,7a Apollo House, Calleva Park
Aldermaston, Berks, RG7 8TN**

Title	Price	Quantity	Value
Channel Islands	£6.99	....	....
Devon & Cornwall	£4.95	....	....
Dorset, Hants & Isle of Wight	£4.95	....	....
East Anglia	£4.95	....	....
Gloucestershire	£6.99	....	....
Heart of England	£4.95	....	....
Lancashire & Cheshire	£4.95	....	....
Lake District & Cumbria	£4.95	....	....
North Wales	£4.95	....	....
Northumberland & Durham	£4.95	....	....
Peak District	£6.99	....	....
Potteries	£6.99	....	....
Somerset	£6.99	....	....
South East	£4.95	....	....
South Wales	£4.95	....	....
Thames & Chilterns	£5.99	....	....
Welsh Borders	£5.99	....	....
Wiltshire	£6.99	....	....
Yorkshire & Humberside	£4.95	....	....
England	£9.99	....	....
Ireland	£8.99	....	....
Scotland	£8.99	....	....
Wales	£8.99	....	....
TOTAL			

**For orders of less than 10 copies please add £1 per book for
postage & packing. Orders over 10 copies P & P free.**

I enclose a cheque for £ .... made payable to Travel
Publishing Ltd

NAME ....

ADDRESS ....

....

POSTCODE ....

TEL NO ....

The Hidden Places Series
READER REACTION FORM

The Hidden Places research team would like to receive reader's comments on any visitor attractions or places reviewed in the book and also recommendations for suitable entries to be included in the next edition. This will help ensure that the ***Hidden Places*** series continues to provide its readers with useful information on the more interesting, unusual or unique features of each attraction or place ensuring that their stay in the local area is an enjoyable and stimulating experience.

To provide your comments or recommendations would you please complete the forms below as indicated and send to: **The Research Department, Travel Publishing Ltd., 7a Apollo House, Calleva Park, Aldermaston, Reading, RG7 8TN.**

Please tick as appropriate: Comments ☐   Recommendation ☐

Name of *"Hidden Place"*:

Address:

Telephone Number:

Name of Contact:

Comments/Reason for recommendation:

Name of Reader:

Address:

Telephone Number:

The Hidden Places Series
READER REACTION FORM

The Hidden Places research team would like to receive reader's comments on any visitor attractions or places reviewed in the book and also recommendations for suitable entries to be included in the next edition. This will help ensure that the **Hidden Places** series continues to provide its readers with useful information on the more interesting, unusual or unique features of each attraction or place ensuring that their stay in the local area is an enjoyable and stimulating experience.

To provide your comments or recommendations would you please complete the forms below as indicated and send to: **The Research Department, Travel Publishing Ltd., 7a Apollo House, Calleva Park, Aldermaston, Reading, RG7 8TN.**

Please tick as appropriate: Comments ☐   Recommendation ☐

Name of *"Hidden Place"*:

Address:

Telephone Number:

Name of Contact:

Comments/Reason for recommendation:

Name of Reader:

Address:

Telephone Number:

The Hidden Places Series
READER REACTION FORM

The Hidden Places research team would like to receive reader's comments on any visitor attractions or places reviewed in the book and also recommendations for suitable entries to be included in the next edition. This will help ensure that the ***Hidden Places*** series continues to provide its readers with useful information on the more interesting, unusual or unique features of each attraction or place ensuring that their stay in the local area is an enjoyable and stimulating experience.

To provide your comments or recommendations would you please complete the forms below as indicated and send to: **The Research Department, Travel Publishing Ltd., 7a Apollo House, Calleva Park, Aldermaston, Reading, RG7 8TN.**

Please tick as appropriate: Comments ☐ Recommendation ☐

Name of *"Hidden Place"*:

Address:

Telephone Number:

Name of Contact:

Comments/Reason for recommendation:

Name of Reader:

Address:

Telephone Number:

The Hidden Places Series
READER REACTION FORM

The Hidden Places research team would like to receive reader's comments on any visitor attractions or places reviewed in the book and also recommendations for suitable entries to be included in the next edition. This will help ensure that the *Hidden Places* series continues to provide its readers with useful information on the more interesting, unusual or unique features of each attraction or place ensuring that their stay in the local area is an enjoyable and stimulating experience.

To provide your comments or recommendations would you please complete the forms below as indicated and send to: **The Research Department, Travel Publishing Ltd., 7a Apollo House, Calleva Park, Aldermaston, Reading, RG7 8TN.**

Please tick as appropriate: Comments ☐ Recommendation ☐

Name of *"Hidden Place"*:

Address:

Telephone Number:

Name of Contact:

Comments/Reason for recommendation:

Name of Reader:

Address:

Telephone Number:

The Hidden Places Series
READER REACTION FORM

The Hidden Places research team would like to receive reader's comments on any visitor attractions or places reviewed in the book and also recommendations for suitable entries to be included in the next edition. This will help ensure that the **Hidden Places** series continues to provide its readers with useful information on the more interesting, unusual or unique features of each attraction or place ensuring that their stay in the local area is an enjoyable and stimulating experience.

To provide your comments or recommendations would you please complete the forms below as indicated and send to: **The Research Department, Travel Publishing Ltd., 7a Apollo House, Calleva Park, Aldermaston, Reading, RG7 8TN.**

Please tick as appropriate: Comments ☐   Recommendation ☐

Name of *"Hidden Place"*: _____

Address: _____

Telephone Number: _____

Name of Contact: _____

Comments/Reason for recommendation: _____

Name of Reader: _____

Address: _____

Telephone Number: _____

Map Section

The following pages of maps encompass the main cities, towns and geographical features of Wiltshire, as well as all the many interesting places featured in the guide. Distances are indicated by the use of scale bars located below each of the maps

Map Key

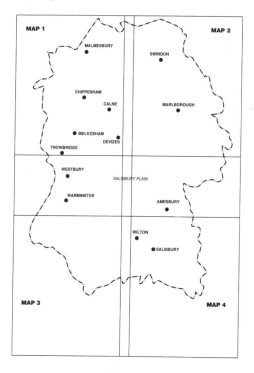

These maps are small scale extracts from the *Wessex Official Tourist Map*, reproduced with kind permission of *Estates Publications*.

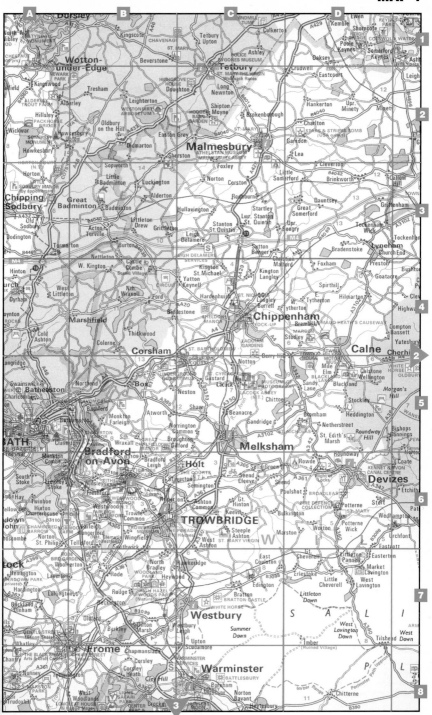

MAP 1

MAP 2

MAP 3

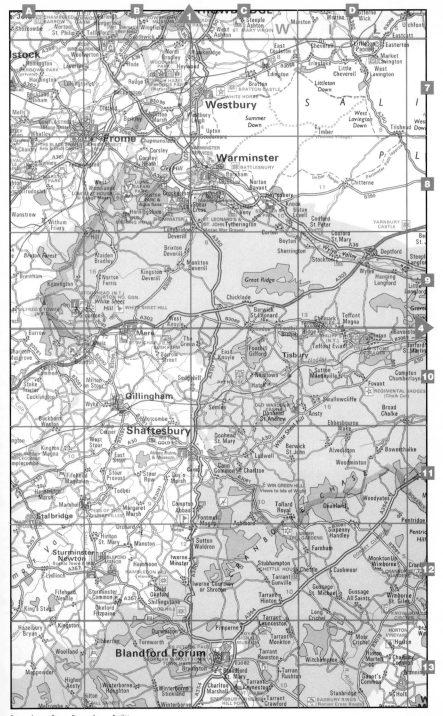

MAP 4

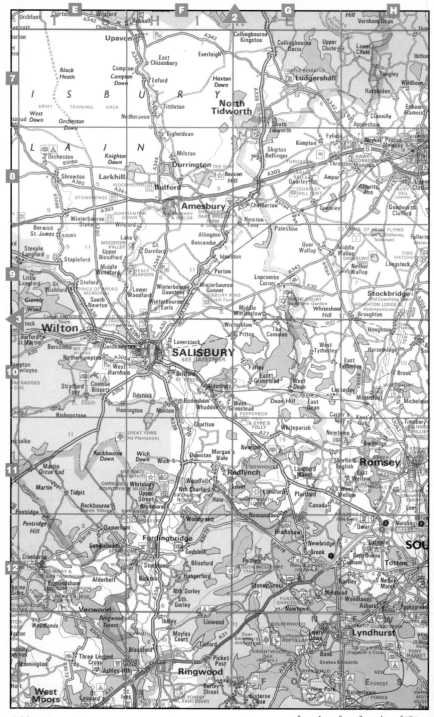

©*Estate Publications* *Crown Copyright Reserved*